SPIRITS & SORROW

Amanda L. Foster

Copyright © 2024 by Amanda L Foster

All rights reserved.

No part of this publication may be reproduced, distributed, or transmitted in any form or by any means, including photocopying, recording, or other electronic or mechanical methods, without the prior written permission of the publisher, except as permitted by UK copyright law. For permission requests, contact Amanda at amanda@zerofierce.com or via her website at:

https://www.zerofierce.com

For privacy reasons, some names, locations, and dates may have been changed.

Book Cover by Amanda Foster

Spirits & Sorrow / Amanda Foster First edition 2024

Chapter Design by Freepik.

ISBN No. 9798327785434

For Steve, Daniel, Levi & Charlie.

My World x

Table of Contents

FORWARD *By Annie Grace* 7

Introduction 12

Chapter One *How it all began* 22

Chapter Two *F.I.N.E.* 30

Chapter Three *The only way is through* 42

Chapter Four *Why alcohol helps, and why it hinders, during a life-changing event* 50

Chapter Five *Understanding what alcohol does to numb you* 59

Chapter Six *Versions of You* 72

Chapter Seven *Events and Socialising without alcohol* 86

Chapter Eight *Tactics to help if it gets difficult* 107

Chapter Nine *What To Do If Your Partner Still Drinks* 119

Chapter Ten *What to do instead of grabbing a drink* 136

Chapter Eleven *Moderation, and moving on* 154

Chapter Twelve *Putting It All Together And Further Help* 176

Free Resources 180

End Credits 184

About The Author 188

FORWARD

By Annie Grace

First of all, I am sorry for your loss. There is nothing harder then losing someone who you love so much. Right now you want to be gentle with yourself and treat yourself with grace.

The one thing I know from personal experience, is that the only way, is through. The more we can experience grief, express it, feel it, allow it to run through us in its fullest, the more that it changes inside of us. There is a saying:

"Every feeling, fully felt, changes."

This does not mean everything can change back to being the same. However when you allow these feelings to run the course freely, it does mean you can experience change that, while altering you profoundly, leaves you in a transformative place. Your experiences can help you to be of service to the world in some way that will transform not only your own life, but that of others going through the same thing as you.

Drinking alcohol is the wrong tool when you are grieving, because it allows none of this to happen. Societal beliefs do not help either, because we are trained not to cry at funerals, or to always hide our grief. It is so important to give yourself permission to grieve fully, and not to feel any shame about it.

Why do grief and alcohol tend to go together?

Dr. Kevin McCauley says we have something called a hedonic threshold. The hedonic threshold can be looked at in the same way as your body temperature. You have a threshold where we're trying to maintain a natural sense of well-being and if you are fall below your threshold you can do things to bring yourself back up. So many studies show that real addiction can be born from times of severe pain, trauma, grief and stress. That is why grief and alcohol can go together.

For most of us drinking was really something that was more or less take it or leave it until something happened, such as losing someone we love. It wasn't always a specific pinpoint moment but until life got stressful and something happened where all of a sudden drinking started to be something that you did for for stress and for self medication and that was really where drinking alcohol took off. Left unchecked, it can be very hard to stop.

A friend of mine was not all that bothered with drinking, until she broke up with her partner, which caused her a huge amount of stress and emotional unhappiness. When she poured a glass of wine she noticed drinking it felt different to her when she was stressed. It helped her feel less alone.

For me, it was just after my second son was born. I was working in a high-powered, executive level job, travelling twice a week internationally, and I was away from my kids all the time. I got on a plane when my son was only six weeks old, which was incredibly stressful for me. I now recognise that as a point in time when drinking became more than just drinking with friends. It became something that I felt I needed.

This sort of story has come up over and over again as the entry point to alcohol dependence. Stress and anxiety increases your chance of becoming addicted to the substance. It can also be seen in people with very traumatic childhoods, or stressful periods of their teenage years, when that first drink they take is the first time they feel 'normal'. In these circumstances they can become addicted very quickly.

Your hedonic threshold can be likened to you getting a fever. Your body temperature needs to kill off the bug, so the temperature of your whole body rises. Your body is now operating at a much higher temperature than it normally would.

Your emotions are the same. So if your thoughts, feelings and emotions fall below the 50% line, and you feel anxious, stressed or upset, your body will try its best to get back to a normal level. If you are drinking wine, then your brain may decide this is what it needs to return you to a calmer state of being. Of course, healthier options would be to walk the dog, or have a cup of tea and read for a little while.

Alcohol and your brain during the grieving process

When you are experiencing abnormal levels of stress and anxiety, for example when you are grieving the loss of a loved one, your threshold for your wellbeing rises to a much higher level, a bit like your temperature does when you have a fever. Which means, all of sudden, something like a cup of tea and book no longer make you feel better. You cannot go for a walk and get over the loss of a loved one.

And this is where addictive substances such as alcohol can take hold, because they become useful. They release artificial levels of dopamine, the learning molecule. This huge spike in dopamine can break through to the upper hedonic level, where grief resides, and make the person feel a little better for a short time. Your brain learns this worked, because dopamine tells us what to do next, and requests more of it.

Your brain learned that the addictive substance brought you back up to your wellbeing level, even through grief. It has decided, that this thing - alcohol - is important for your survival. It will begin to demand this substance over everything. Over eating healthily, over drinking water, over socialising, over everything.

Your brain is trying to look after you, but it is recommending the wrong tool for your survival. You will hear more about this later in this book, as it is an important factor taught to all my students in the This Naked Mind Institute.

So, be very gentle with yourself right now. Love yourself. Take care of yourself above everything else. Think of it as doing a service to yourself to go through this as much as possible without numbing yourself with alcohol. Allow yourself to feel the love for those you lost, in its purest form, even if it feels intolerable sometimes. The last thing your loved one wants is for an addiction to be borne from this tragedy.

The only way, is through.

Annie Grace

Founder of This Naked Mind, &

Author, *This Naked Mind: Control Alcohol, Find Freedom, Discover Happiness & Change Your Life.*

INTRODUCTION

"Alcohol erases a bit of you every time you drink it. It can even erase entire nights when you are on a binge. Alcohol does not relieve stress; it erases your senses and your ability to think. Alcohol ultimately erases your self."

— Annie Grace, This Naked Mind

Have you have experienced the loss of a loved one? If so, then the above quote by Annie Grace may resonate strongly with you. It does for me. It is the quote I come back to time and time again in my role as an Alcohol Freedom Coach.

At my lowest point I was deliberately erasing my senses and my ability to think. I did not want to think about anything that was going on around me. I drank every single night to numb my feelings. It felt as though I had discovered the perfect tool in which to hide.

For me, the last part of the quote never came to pass. "Alcohol ultimately erases your self." It did not erase me. And do you want to know why?

Because I did not allow it to. I fought back, with the tools I am about to show you. Another part of the reason is because I read the book, *This Naked Mind*, from which the quote above came from. Spooky, eh? I am continually astounded by the life I discovered after I had stopped drowning my sorrows in alcohol. I found me again. I honestly thought she was lost forever.

With alcohol gone from my mind and my life, I decided wanted to give something back. So I trained as a Certified Coach with the This Naked Mind Institute, which was born from the success of Annie's book. I had to show the whole world how incredible life can be without alcohol. Even after huge, life-shattering loss. Even after losing a child, parent, sibling, or best friend.

Right now, we are at the centre of a global epidemic. Alcohol is cheaper than it has ever been. It is more easily accessed than it has ever been. It is more heavily marketed than it has ever been. And these three things make it more insidious than it has ever been.

This book is especially for those who have fallen into the alcohol trap following the loss of a loved one. I loved a quit-lit book when I was giving up. But there was nothing for grief out there for me. It is for anyone who has experienced grief, and decided alcohol is a great way to lose yourself. To drown out the pain. You may have only just started drinking, or maybe you have been stuck in a repetitive cycle for a while. Perhaps you have realised you are finding it harder than you expected to control your drinking.

I understand what you are going through. I am here now to show you hope through my stories, my experiences, and the tools and tactics I learned at the Institute. I am here to guide you out of the hole you might find yourself. Or at least join you, sit beside you for a while, and show you some alternative options.

I want to show you there is an easier way to go through your grief. It may even shorten your journey, and even improve it for you and everyone around you, as it did for me. Grief is necessary because you loved the person you lost so deeply. Lengthening it is unnecessary. It only hurts for longer, and your loved one would hate to think you were causing yourself harm or further pain in their name.

Big alcohol brands are brilliant at marketing alcohol, and they spend billions every year showing us what a great time you can have with their brand of beer, gin, rum, wine or vodka. The marketing machine hits us from all sides - battering us with messages in the movies or TV shows we watch, TV adverts, billboards, social media and digital advertising. They all show us one thing: Escapism.

If you are grieving the loss of someone you cared for deeply, this escapism from the norm can be incredibly tempting. Add gifts from well-wishers such as our friends and family, and the societal acceptance of alcohol, and you have a powerful mix, a vortex, even, into which we can disappear for a while and escape our sadness. The dopamine hit it provides allows us a reprieve from the constant ache of loss and pain our loved one has left behind.

The issue, of course, is that alcohol is one of the most addictive substances on the planet. Yes, more addictive than smoking, more addictive than even the worst of drugs.

So, when we try to control it, or try to escape the trap, we find ourselves ever more stuck and unable to free ourselves. Sometimes we are unable to free ourselves until something awful happens, or until we hit 'rock bottom'.

I am here to tell you there is no need to wait until that happens. You can get out now, without further misery, without white-knuckling it or using willpower. You can be free. Forever, if you wish. And this simple guide is going to show you how to get the results you want, quickly, and without fuss. I have distilled the tactics, hacks and tools that helped me and countless others free themselves from alcohol, so that you can smash through all your fears and concerns. So you can start to live your best life ever.

Who is this book for?

You are in the right place if you have lost someone you care about and have used alcohol to hide from your pain.

Perhaps your drinking started innocently enough. You drank with friends and family or at social occasions. Later you started to drink at home, at first with family or friends, and later, alone.

If you started to look forward to the time you could pour yourself a drink, be it after the work day has ended, or at 7pm, or when the kids have gone to bed. Maybe it started as a weekend thing, and then became almost a nightly habit. And maybe this was okay for a while and you had no issues with it. You enjoyed the numbing effect of alcohol and you started to relax as it began to take effect.

Later, perhaps you started to worry about your drinking. It started with a niggling doubt when you discovered you are probably drinking over the "government safe limit". (Tip: There is no safe limit. More on that later on though.)

Maybe you started to make attempts to cut back, or take a break, only to drink even more afterwards when you went back to moderating. Maybe you have even started to experience blackouts where you cannot remember the movie you watched the previous night, or what happened during a social event you attended. Perhaps you have started to experience memory gaps here and there.

You are not alone. Excessive alcohol consumption is a growing the world over.

This is book is for you if you want to do something about it. If you are tired of a few drops of alcohol having so much power over you and your life. If you crave change, but you are unsure where to start. And if you need support while you are still grieving your lost loved ones. You are in the right place.

Who am I and why have I written this?

You might be asking yourself: "Who is this Amanda person, and why is she speaking to me about this?" And you would be right to ask.

I am a Mum of three boys, and I am in my fifties. I started losing people close to me pretty early on. Dad died at 27. My 12 year old son died when I was 32. He was my first born. I also lost my Mum early, and my lovely brother. And some amazing friends too. I would have loved to have written my first book about something cool, like space, or unicorns, but here we are. It turns out I am particularly well-positioned to write about grief of the worst kind. I also disappeared into alcohol in an attempt to hide from grief, and then I carried on drinking to hide from stress and the pain that followed grief. And I struggled, badly, to break free.

But then a few years ago something amazing happened. It was like magic, but actually, it was more like tapping into my subconscious thoughts and emotions, challenging those beliefs and everything I thought to be true, and coming up with a different answer. And suddenly, I was free.

To say my life changed for the better is a massive understatement. It was exponentially better in ways I could never have imagined.

With my newfound freedom fighting powers, I decided to train as an alcohol and addiction freedom coach. I learned how to use the very same tactics and strategies to help other people who had started to hide from their problems using alcohol or other addictive substances. Those people who find they drink too much, get into arguments they do not want to have, drink more than they would like to, and wake up with their hearts pounding at 3am. Those who cannot remember what happened the previous evening. I also decided I wanted to challenge societal beliefs about those who decide not to drink, and to challenge the fact alcohol is everywhere, on adverts, on TV, in front of our children, despite being addictive and a substance that kills people in their prime. And so ZeroFierce was born.

And now I want to pull back the curtain, *Wizard of Oz* style. I want to expose alcohol for what it really is, and what it does to those who are going through a tough time, or grieving. Someone like you.

I want to give you hope. And I want to tell you that things will get better. And then I want to give you the map with which to escape, and find yourself again. And I want to show you that you are most definitely not alone.

What you're going to learn

Everyone experiences grief in different ways. That being said, there are similarities in so many of my clients stories and my own story, especially when its comes to alcohol and using it to numb grief or hide from a life you would rather not be facing at the time.

In **Chapters 1 and 2** I am going to tell you how my story started, and when alcohol became more than a night out with friends. How I gave it a job, just as many of us do when we decide to use it as a crutch.

In Chapter 3 I am going to look at the complexities of grief and alcohol, how the mix can be so toxic it can actually compound our problems and make everything feel so much worse. You may be familiar with some of the effects yourself, so I am hoping it will speak to you and show you I understand. But I am not going to ignore the fact that alcohol can, in some ways, assist us in the grieving process, or when we are very unhappy, stressed or depressed.

In Chapter 4 we will look at how it helps, how it hinders, and everything in-between. This is also where I introduce you to the first of our tactics, and hope, especially if you are feeling trapped or unable to easily give up alcohol for more than a few days or a month.

In Chapter 5 we will touch very lightly on the science side of what alcohol actually does to us as the addiction intensifies, and why you are struggling to stop drinking or control alcohol. Don't worry, it's very light, there are plenty of science-led quit-lit books around and that is not what I am here for. It is also super interesting, and it will show you that none of this is your fault. Yep! None of it. *You are not an alcoholic.*

In Chapter 6 I introduce some reflective thinking. This helped me enormously when I was going through my own journey. I hope you enjoy this one - it has worked well on clients and colleagues alike, and is great fun to do. I highly recommend you write your own version after reading this chapter. It can be so powerful. It really awakens your subconscious mind to the possibilities you might be missing out on.

In Chapter 7 we will address a few of your concerns you might be struggling with. Sometimes you might not even be aware you are worried about these things until faced with the idea of losing them. To take a break from alcohol is actually pretty badass. You are going against the social norm, and some people may struggle with your decision. This chapter will counter all the biggest concerns we see from clients, and give you the confidence to challenge your thoughts and emotions on the subject.

Chapter 8 will focus on some of my top tactics. They helped me, and they have helped tens of thousands of people all over the world to find freedom from alcohol - whether it is to get it back under control, or to give it up entirely. Some, like me, never want to drink alcohol again. Imagine that! We also look at how important it is to self-care during this period of change. When you strip away alcohol there is nowhere left to hide, so it can get pretty intense. But I promise you it can be intense in a good way. In a healthy way. Get excited, because good things are coming your way.

Chapter 9 looks at your relationships, and particularly addresses something that crops up time and time again in my line of work. Something I have experienced personally, too. What to do if your partner still drinks, and how to handle this and other situations around you. I have some brilliant, tried and tested tactics in here as well for just about every eventuality. We also look again at alcohol and how it can hinder the grieving process. You will find I repeat some points occasionally, but this is because they are important. Repetition works on your subconscious thoughts. In fact, my breakthrough with alcohol actually happened on my second reading of the books I had previously read. The first time chipped away at things I thought were true. The second time smashed those ideas and mistaken truths apart. Just like magic.

In Chapter 10 we'll look at your daily activity and things you can do to replace the drinking part of your life in order to make this change easier. Without drink you will find yourself having more time (and money) on your hands. Here is a fun part where we explore all the things you can do with this extra time. Hint: It's pretty unlimited, so this is a great place to get to.

Chapter 11 explores moderation, and whether you should consider it. It is entirely your choice, but I will address the pros and cons of moderation, and also list some of the unexpected, wonderful things you might miss out on if you decide this is what you want to do. Hopefully you can make an informed choice that is personal to you.

Finally, Chapter 12 looks at further resources. Whether you need extra support, or just want to deep dive into this incredible new life you have discovered, this is the perfect chapter for looking at where you go from here.

It is my hope that this book helps you, even if it's just a little. Because if it does, then I have achieved my goal. This was my deepest desire from the minute I discovered how amazing our lives can be, with alcohol in check, even after losing those we love the most.

Stay strong, my friend, have hope, and read on. I have so much to show you.

Ok! So now you know where we are going. Let's get started, shall we?

See you on the other side.

Amanda x

Chapter One

How it all began

The Beginning

"It is by going down into the abyss that we recover the treasures of life. Where you stumble, there lies your treasure."

— Joseph Campbell

If you are a parent, you might know about that nagging feeling you get sometimes when something is not quite right with one of your kids. Perhaps you were occasionally proven right. Several times, when Daniel was too quiet, I would creep up to the room he was playing in, and slowly, quietly, move my head around the doorway to see what he was up to. Sure enough, there he was, drawing a dinosaur on the wall in the living room. The newly painted wall…

"Daniel!" I barked, and he jumped a mile vertically, face and ears reddening, eyes darting around guiltily, as he threw the crayon into the toy box beside him.

My mouth struggled to stay straight as I tried not to laugh. Hoping my eyes were serious, I glared at him.

"Sorry Mum", he said, woefully, "I'll clean it off."

"Ok. Get a sponge from the kitchen, and some washing up liquid." I replied, and sat down on the sofa and opened my book.

As I watched him try to scrub the crayon off the wall, I marvelled at how perfect this little human being was. He had the cutest haircut, the bluest of eyes, and the cheekiest of cheeky grins. He was bold charactered and strong-willed. I was occasionally told he was "difficult" at school, because he saw the funny side of everything, and would have the classroom in peels of laughter when they should have been learning. However the teachers liked him, and he was a bright and a good natured little soul. I felt very fortunate.

One day, when he was out with friends, I felt a strange lurch in my heart, and sure enough shortly after this one of his friends knocked on the front door. As soon as I answered the door he blurted, out of breath, that Daniel had been "riding" a shopping trolley in the streets, and it had fallen, tossing him out of it, and they were worried he had broken his ankle. As I raced to him, with his friend showing me the way, I could see at the end of the street there was a crumpled heap of shopping trolley and two children scattered on the pavement.

Daniel was in obvious pain as I approached, as was another of his friends, so I had to go back and get my car to take them both to casualty. As it turned out, nothing was broken, but Daniel had sprained his ankle and knee pretty badly, so he was off his feet for at least a week.

"Twerps." I told the kids, rolling my eyes at them. The kids laughed and chattered excitedly about their adventure, telling me about the somersaults they had taken before landing on the pavement as the trolley sped out of control. Back then I hardly worried about the kids. They were simply experiencing the freedom I had myself experienced as a child, growing up in Oxford. And kids were made of rubber, weren't they. They always bounced back, I mused to myself.

I hardly recognise that person now.

Daniel was a keen footballer, and played for the local junior team every week. As his biggest supporter, I was able to spend time at the local football ground watching him play, or going to matches to see the main team play. They were pretty high up in the league, so it was great to get free tickets to see a match. I took Daniel to his first ever football game - his dad not being a fan of football - and his face lit up like a Christmas tree. It was a fantastic match, the result was one-nil, and it was a hard-fought win. His passion grew and grew, and soon he was playing in a forward position for the junior team.

He would even play five a side with his father sometimes, amongst adults. They would all tell me afterwards that he was absolutely fearless, tackling even the tallest men with bravado. He was so bold and brave, and he adored playing football more than anything.

Alongside all the football, naturally, came injuries. Nothing major, but a lot of twisted ankles and knees, grazes, cuts and bruises. One particularly rough game with his team caused a knee injury, and Daniel missed out on an important match. He was destitute, but he knew the importance of recovery after each injury, and knew he needed to be patient before playing again.

Except, this knee injury did not seem to go away like the others had. It plagued him for weeks. I had to take him back to the GP and the physio a few times to get it checked out. They gave him the all clear, each time. They had no concerns. But they told him to rest it up, give it another week, no football allowed.

Another couple of weeks went by, and by now he was asking for painkillers at night because the pain would wake him up, or even stop him falling asleep.

"Growing pains." The doctor declared. I nodded - I had suffered from them myself.

A couple of weeks later, Daniel came down the stairs at 11pm, complaining of pain in his leg. I felt something shift in my chest. Something wasn't right. Maybe that football injury had caused something to dislodge. I decided that the local doctor wasn't helping - I wanted his leg X-rayed by someone who knew about football injuries. By now Daniel was desperate to go back to playing football, and he was getting frustrated by the lack of progress on his injury too.

The following morning, first thing, we drove to the local hospital Accident and Emergency Unit.

After explaining the issue, he was examined by a triage nurse.

"There's nothing wrong with him, he is moving it fine." She informed me.

Firmly I said: "If you don't mind, I will wait for a doctor and an X-ray please. He is complaining of pain quite a bit now. Pretty much every night."

"We are very busy, so it will be a long wait." She replied.

"Yes, yes, that's fine." I said. "We will wait."

So we sat there, for over seven hours, watching as every child went ahead of Daniel, with me absorbing the glares from the triage nurse occasionally. Even a tiny bumped head, and toothache, took precedence. It was clear they wanted us to go home. But that was okay, the children were younger than my 11 year old boy, so we waited. We didn't care, we laughed and joked, and Daniel told me stories about school. He never stopped talking, I loved his energy.

The triage nurse left, replaced by another, and we waited for another hour as every single other child went through. Finally, when there were no more children to be seen, the nurse approached us.

"There doesn't seem to be anything wrong with your son, Mrs Foster." He said.

"Please, we have waited all day. Can you just not give him a quick X-ray?" I pleaded.

"It's really busy today, you should go home and make an appointment with your GP." He replied.

"I am happy to wait." I said. "I have seen the GP over and over again, and it is not healing. I am having to give him painkillers just to be able to sleep. Surely that is not right?"

He stared at me blankly.

"I know he looks fine, but I am telling you, he is not. I will wait, thank you." I said firmly, and I went back to my book. There was no way I would leave having been there all day. I wanted answers.

"Fine! Follow me" he grumbled, and we followed him into the next area where he booked the X-ray.

As we waited for the results Daniel and I laughed and joked about bits falling off him, and him going radiation green. He laughed so hard, and I felt better now that we had finally had the Xray and someone could see if anything was broken or fractured.

Three doctors approached us. Their faces stern. They introduced themselves to me and Daniel in turn, and we both laughed at the severity of the situation. "Uh oh Mum, I have no-legged-itis. It's serious!" He cried - dramatically fake dying into the waiting room chair. I laughed, but the doctors faces stayed grim. At that point I had not trained myself to spot things like that, I was so free from all things medically scary, but looking back on it afterwards the warning signs were all there.

"We think Daniel may have a tumour." one of them said, soberly.

"Oh, okay, how do we fix that?" I asked brightly.

A look passed between them all. They looked surprised.

"Erm, well, we have to do some tests, and maybe a biopsy, and then we can do a treatment plan once we know what we are dealing with."

"Okay. So it IS No-legged-itis." I said nervously, and winked at Daniel. I had no idea what a biopsy was. No idea what a tumour was. Daniel laughed again and dove into the chair again dramatically.

"Would you mind if I call someone?" I asked the doctors. By now the atmosphere was making me feel dizzy. I needed to know what a tumour was, urgently.

"Sure, absolutely, Daniel, why don't you come with me and I can show you how to use the stethoscope?" the kindly doctor with the nice face said. I nodded, and walked quickly out of the room and across the hall to a payphone.

I started dialling my mum's number, who used to be a nurse before specialising in dementia, so she was the perfect person to ask. I waited for her soothing voice to respond. You always need your Mum when things are tough, don't you?

"Eight One Nine Eight Hundred" she said over the phone piece. I loved that she answered the phone with her number.

"Mum? Mum I am at the hospital. What's a tumour?" I asked, my voice wobbling with concern.

My Mum's voice went stern and serious. Looking back now, this alone reported back to me the nature of the issue was pretty bad. Mum was never stern.

"Why? What's wrong?"

I garbled out what had happened that day, and the reason I was there, and I started to cry. I did not know why.

"Okay, Amanda, call Steve. I'll be there later today. I'm coming."

I hung up on my Mum to call Steve, my husband. Pushing another fifty pence into the payphone, my heart pounding, I knew by now something was very, very wrong. My mum lived over 400 miles away, had recently lost my Dad to a heart attack. And she loathed driving long distances.

My husband answered the phone with a silly pet name he often used for me. I ignored him and said:

"Steve, drop Levi off to your Mum, you need to get to the hospital. I don't know what is happening. I think they are saying Daniel might be very sick."

Chapter Two

F.I.N.E.

"The best way out is always through."

— Robert Frost

My drinking journey started long before all of this happened, but overall it was pretty harmless. It certainly wasn't every night. I would binge drink a little perhaps when I went out with friends, no more than anyone else in the nineties though. I was more interested in going clubbing at the time, and I loved to drive a minibus full of our friends to clubs all over the UK on nights out, so drinking did not really mix with my idea of fun nights. I loved to dance, too, and we all know how that goes when we are drunk.

Basically, I had not yet given alcohol a 'job' to do. And for as long as that is true, your drinking can often stay controllable. I did not crave it, I drank it maybe every couple of weeks. It was fine.

My Dad died, aged 51, when I was 27. It was the same year my husband lost one of his best friends. I have that year marked as one of the worst years in my life for sure. I was so close to Dad, he was the best Dad ever. He died at work, of a heart attack, I was told. I was devastated, and my drinking increased a little. I started drinking at home for a bit, to wash away the grief. It was then that I had given alcohol a job - to numb the pain. The addiction cycle started, and my drinking increased to drinking at home while playing PC games, or watching TV, or studying.

I saw no harm in my alcohol consumption, though. All of my gaming friends drank, and it was causing me no real harm. I functioned fine, I worked hard, I was successful at my job, and I was a good Mum to my two beautiful boys. I had a nice life, by all regards, and I was happy. Sure, I probably drank a bit too much, but I think we all did back then. It was fine.

It frightens me sometimes when I realise that Dad died over twenty five years ago. By the time I stopped drinking alcohol, I had been drinking nightly for well over two decades. Twenty Five years. Count them.

I'll take you back to that fateful day first though… bear with me here, I want to get it out and on paper and over with. As you can imagine, this is very painful to write. But it's important you know my "why".

It took three more weeks before the biopsy could be carried out, and then another three weeks before they had the results. I reached the hospital first. My husband and I were advised to be there together, so my heart was pounding as I sat alone. When Steve finally arrived both he and I were quickly ferried to a room in the hospital that looked a bit like my Nan's house. It was private, and was free from the medical paraphernalia and posters that adorned the walls of the rest of the building. We sat on the sofa as one of the consultants stood before us.

It was serious. He had only seen it once before, a long time ago, and it was identical. It was a rare form of cancer that attacked the joints, often in teenagers, called Osteosarcoma. The biopsy was clear, and there would be lots of new tests, and now they would be able to draw up an action plan. But the consultant said that despite the small chance of survival, they would attack the cancer proactively, removing the knee and replacing it with a titanium version, and there would be several rounds of chemotherapy. Sadly it was a super aggressive cancer, so they had to check it had not travelled elsewhere, which, if it had, would lower Daniel's chance of survival even further. This would mean that Daniel would need an incredibly aggressive form of chemo treatment, and a rocky ride was expected for him.

As he left the room, Steve and I sat in stunned silence.

I have no idea why, but my next words out of my mouth were:

"Well, we will have to get rid of the dog. This is napalm!" And I burst into tears. I guess it was the shock.

I was right about the second thing at least, but our German Shepherd, Chloe, stayed with Daniel, and was a huge joy to us all until her eventual death at 14, many years after this part of the story ends. Beautiful girl.

That was the last time I cried for a long, long time. Oh, how I used to fight those tears, and stay brave. If you take one piece of advice from this book, then please, cry as much as you want to, and let those tears flow freely, for as long as you need them to. They are there for a reason. I had no idea back then, I thought it was my job to be brave for everyone. But of course, as the main carer during Daniels treatment, I had to maintain a positive presence for him. Those were the last sober tears I cried for decades. The rest were all numbed by alcohol, along with the pain. The problem is if you numb the bad stuff, you also numb all the good stuff…

Treatment started for Daniel, and we approached it with gusto. Daniel was so brave, mature well beyond his eleven years, and tried to stay bright. But the treatment was absolutely brutal.

The chemo made him very ill, and they removed his knee and replaced it with a titanium knee. A few weeks into the treatment they discovered the cancer had already spread into his shoulder too, but it was not as advanced, so they removed bone from his shin on the other leg and grafted it into his shoulder. He had all of these operations done in one go, because the window between chemotherapy treatments was so small. So by the time they had finished with him in surgery, it was like he had been hit by a bus.

I stayed in one of the rooms provided by the local children's cancer charity, so I was able to travel all over the country to the various hospitals in London and Southampton with Daniel, and stay overnight with him each time. I made friends with other parents in the same situation, and we would look after our kids by day, and then go back to the house and drink together in the evenings, sharing our feelings, our fears and our stories. We thought the alcohol would help us release the stresses and horrors of the day, and then it helped us into a dreamless sleep at night, so we were able to start it all again the following day. It was a treadmill, a painful one for our children, filled with a lot of appointments and racing around various hospitals, and not a lot of hope. This went on for Daniel and I for eight to ten months, which allowed my alcohol drinking to become a full-blown habit, unbeknownst to me at the time. I sleep-walked my way into addiction.

You might be wondering, how do you know when you are starting to use alcohol to numb grief or pain?

Well, the markers are not easy to see, especially if you are hurting, and the climb into addiction is insidious. I can tell you about a few I spotted, though.

First of all, it is when alcohol starts to creep up in importance during your evening. If you are getting through the day, and then find yourself thinking about the time you can have a glass of wine, or a beer, to "relax", this can be a sign it is starting.

For me, this started when I was staying at Stanmore Hospital in London. Daniel had finished his surgery, and the prognosis was still not good, as recent scans had identified tiny, but definite, cancerous spots on his lungs. It was hard to stay positive, and keep up the illusion of bravado, as it was. But by now I knew it was probably pretty much game over. I could tell by the way the doctors spoke to me. Their manner had changed completely, and they would speak in hushed whispers around us, never quite looking either of us in the eye. I tried very hard to ignore them, but I was not always successful, and occasional bouts of rage would implode inside me. It was so unfair! He was just a gorgeous, innocent child. Why was this happening to him?

The bottle of drink in the tiny room I was staying in at the crumbling hospital was the only way out for me. The roof leaked every time it rained. Late every evening I would go back, drink a few drinks - not huge amounts, but enough to numb the pain and anger, which would allow me to sleep without the horrors of the day repeating themselves as nightmares in my head night after night. I was so alone, as Daniel was mostly out of it on painkillers, so, mercifully, he slept a lot. I would sit beside him all day, occasionally playing console games with him if he woke, or grabbing him tasty treats to try and keep him eating something. But my mind was consumed with when I could be allowed to go back to my little room, alone, to drink, and to disappear. I had no idea back then, but this was probably where I hit the next stage of my addiction. I had given alcohol an even bigger job to do, and now my brain considered it not only necessary, but essential for my wellbeing.

As Daniel recovered slightly from the surgery, he wanted to see my little room with the leaky ceiling. So we wandered over one day to have some lunch together, and to get him out of the ward for a little while. He struggled to get up the rickety stairs with his crutches, but he looked relieved to be free for a while.

As we sat down on the bed, a huge crane fly danced across the window, and slowly danced towards me. I screamed loudly, I hated crane flies most of all! And I ran into the wardrobe and closed the door behind me. As I opened it a tiny crack, I asked Daniel to kill it.

Just like his father, he refused. Instead, he wobbled over to it, enclosed his hands gently over it, and released it out of the little window in the room. He watched as it flew away, and then turned to me. He rolled his eyes at me dramatically.

"Errr, Mum? It's gone. You're safe now." He laughed. "I saved you!"

I laughed and slowly came back out of the wardrobe, peering around the room to make sure there were no more crane flies.

"Thank you, lovely." I replied, and gave him a big hug. "You are my hero!"

He would have made someone an awesome partner in his future, had he have been allowed to have one.

Daniel was almost a teenager, and he did not want his Mum around for everything. When certain checks were needed, he preferred me to leave the area, in order to maintain his dignity. It was all pretty tough on an almost 12 year-old boy. During these times I would sit in the "parents room" and have a coffee with other parents in similar situations to me. All of their children had complex health conditions, but most were not terminally ill, as Daniel now was. I found comfort speaking to these parents. My friends with "healthy" kids were unable to understand most of what I was going through. Or they found it difficult to talk about the things I needed to say. So many nightmarish thoughts rolled around in my brain during that awful time.

One amazing parent taught me the terminology: F.I.N.E.

I asked what I was supposed to say when well-meaning people asked me how I was, but did not want the real answer. They would look at me wide-eyed with shock and fear when I told them the truth. It was a rhetorical question, nobody actually wanted to hear the truth.

"Simple!", she said, "You just tell them you are fine."

The I looked at her quizzically, she explained: "FINE - it stands for "Fucked-Up, Insecure, Neurotic and Emotional. Says it all, doesn't it!"

I laughed, it was perfect! And it gave the person asking the question the reassurance they needed, without the drama, taking the pressure off me to perform, or feel the frustration as I was not being the genuine me.

I will never forget her. She stayed upbeat right until the end. She lost her daughter shortly after I lost Daniel, and disappeared from sight. I think she moved to the North of England to live with her Mum, her marriage in tatters, which is very common when you lose a child, and her daughter being her only child. I hope she is okay now. Or at the very least, I hope she is FINE.

Eventually, we got to the end of the treatment plan. We were all exhausted, especially my beautiful son. He was so excited to get home and just play on his console, and, yes, even go back to school. Despite the fear that he would break his newly fixed shoulder or knee, I allowed him the independence of going back to school alone, although he needed a mobility scooter to travel unaided. His friends all welcomed him back, and Daniel even became a bit of a local celebrity in the city where we lived at the time. He was amiable and polite to everyone, and still had a wicked sense of humour.

With Daniel fiercely protecting his independence it left me alone in my thoughts and feelings, and able to rest a little. But it also left me alone to feel the searing pain as I waited for the prognosis on the treatment. Had it been a success? I knew the chances were tiny, but I had to believe, to HOPE it would work, or I would have never put him through all that awful treatment. I would count the hours every day until everyone was home and I could sink into a bottle of red wine. By this time, I had stopped drinking rum, because it tasted too nice, and switched to wine, the taste of which I had to acclimatise to.

And this, my friend, is another sign you are lurching deeper into addiction. When you flip drinks because you like the taste of one a little too much, into another where perhaps you have not gotten used to the taste. You hope it will naturally lower the amount you can drink.

Do you remember your first taste of alcohol? Disgusting, wasn't it? We curled up our noses, trying not to spit it out. But with people watching we would resist the urge, and we would swallow it. Alcohol was so prolific in our lives, it must be good, right? So we train ourselves to get used to the taste of it, by drinking it more regularly. Can you imagine doing this with liver? Or fish paste? Yuck! This is very much like smoking, another addictive habit, when we cough and splutter our way through the first few. We never stop to think that perhaps this was our amazing body's way of screaming at us to stop! Drinking is so socially acceptable, we all assume we must do it, and so we keep trying to enjoy the taste, until eventually, we do.

Well, you will already know the prognosis was not good. The treatment had completely and utterly failed. The cancer was attacking Daniel even more aggressively, and the chemotherapy had done nothing to help. It had gone metastatic, and there was nothing more to be done. Our world, collapsed. But still, I held strong, I ignored the pain, and I held resolutely positive. Where medicine had failed, we would try other things! Religion, happiness therapies, diet, and other alternative therapies. We were desperate victims to any and all who said they had a cure. I trained myself to clean his central lines, and to administer all the medicines, and to push a feed tube through his nose and into his stomach, all the things I could never do again, in order to keep him out of the hospitals he hated so much. And I ignored the searing pain of injustice I felt for him, covering it up at nights with more and more red wine.

Six months later, Daniel lost his battle against cancer, and passed away peacefully in his own bed. By now he was just twelve years old.

Cancer is an evil foe. By the time it has ripped through your loved ones, you almost pray for the reprieve of death for them. So, after a few weeks, I was fine. They could not hurt my little boy any more. It was over. Silently, people came and removed all the medical paraphernalia from my cupboards, and cleaned away all the equipment such as morphine pumps and feeding bags. I sat on the sofa, watching them, my heart empty and devoid of any feeling whatsoever. I had become so utterly used to shoving my feelings deep down into the pit of my stomach, they were lost to me, at least for now.

Friends and family bustled around me, talking in hushed whispers, occasionally glancing at me. I would give them small smiles back, to reassure them all I was okay. Just tired. So very tired. Daniel's German Shepherd dog, Chloe, would sit beside me on the sofa and snuggle up to me. She missed her best friend badly, and would not eat, and would whine occasionally and watch the front door, waiting for him to come home. Nothing would comfort her, her toys all went ignored in the corner. She just sat with me, and slept a lot.

Daniel's funeral was huge. I had chosen a huge church in our local area, and I was worried it would feel empty. But the whole neighbourhood turned up, along with most of the people from two of his schools, all his friends and their families, shop keepers, teachers, policemen, celebrities… Daniel had touched so many people's hearts.

I stood at the front of the church, heard nothing, felt nothing. I gave people small smiles to reassure them I was okay. And I looked forward to the time I could go home and drink wine to stem the feelings bubbling away under the surface, threatening to consume me. I did not want to exist anymore. I just wanted the beautiful numbness wine would give me.

There you go. Another sign your drinking might be getting out of hand. Wanting to numb everything and anything. Feelings, emotions, thoughts, and the need to even think about the next day. Deliberately drinking as much as possible in order to disappear. Now alcohol has an even bigger job to do.

By this time my drinking had gotten so bad, I would panic if there was less than a bottle of red wine in the house. And then I would panic if there were only two left. I started ordering boxes of wine on subscriptions, and spending more on wine, even buying organic wine, because it felt "healthier". Surely the more it costs, the better it is for us?

I hung on every news story telling me that a glass of wine a day was good for my heart. And so it was! Drinking several glasses a night stopped it hurting so much for four hours a night, before I passed out into a dreamless sleep until the morning. And if there were fewer than two bottles left in the house, I would send people out to buy more. By now wine had become my safety net.

I was still a good parent by day, and great at my job. I was what was called a high-functioning drinker, or grey area drinker, and I was heading into real trouble. But I had no idea. What you don't know, you simply don't know. And I knew nothing about the dangers of alcohol. How could I? It was socially acceptable, and advertised every night on the television as a great source of adult entertainment. It was everywhere. I was surrounded in messages saying it was fine. Everything was just FINE.

Chapter Three

The only way is through

"It's not whether you get knocked down. It's whether you get up."

— Vince Lombardi

Several months after the funeral, things fell back into normality pretty quickly. Almost too quickly, I would say. The worst thing about losing someone close to you, at first, is that life simply trundles on.

Cars will still cut you off at the traffic lights, even though you just lost your son. Bills will still mound up, and bailiffs threaten to take your goods, or your home, even though you just lost your son. And people are rude to you in shops, when you stand staring at the butter aisle for too long, lost in thought, trying to work out why you came to the supermarket in the first place. But you will not necessarily move on, you stay stuck in time, and this is completely and utterly normal. So give yourself plenty of space and compassion, even when it is unavailable from anywhere or anyone else.

I didn't give myself any compassion. I stayed strong. I did not cry, or release my frustration at all. I stayed strong for Levi, my younger son, because this is what I thought I should do. And I stayed strong for my husband, because he was collapsing inwardly with pain and searing hurt, and wanted to fight the world in anger. So I did as many women do, and stayed strong for the family.

And when you do something like this, the damage will be felt elsewhere. It transfers, as it cannot escape where it needs to. You start using things to cope. My coping mechanism was alcohol, and escapism in gaming. If the real world was crap, why live in it? I did my 'Mum duties', and I did my job, and then I disappeared into an online gaming world called Everquest at first, and Eve Online, and then later, World of Warcraft. Those worlds were far more forgiving, and full of good people, who did not know me as "Cancer-Mum". In fact, for several years, I did not even identify myself to my gaming buddies as female. And that world accepted me with open arms, and I got pretty good at the games. So every waking minute of the day when I wasn't being a Mum or working, I lived in those worlds, with my online friends, where it was safe.

Now, you might be thinking that gaming and drinking do not mix, but in fact they mix brilliantly, I soon found out! We would all get absolutely hammered on voice chat, and then go and attack the other faction en masse, collapsing into laughter at funny jokes, and playing late into the night. I made life-long friends on those games. It was a wonderful place, and soon some of my real life friends joined me in there, because that was the only place they could reach me, by now. And there I stayed, for over eight years, and I still play occasionally even now.

In World of Warcraft, the worlds were full of colour and amusing side quests, and lots of team play to get rid of hugely complex foes, with up to forty of our team on a single fight in some cases. After a big fight, I would ride my beautiful animated horse into town, where newer players would private message me on occasion to compliment me on the armour I had bravely won in those same fights. My avatar did look pretty awesome, even if I say so myself! The world was almost solely positive, and death was only temporary. It was the best place for me possible. Cancer did not exist. Just friendship, fun, and a lot of laughter.

After around eight years, I started meeting up with these new friends, visiting Warwick Castle, or Alton Towers Theme Park, and slowly I was reintroduced back into the real world. But while the gaming was fairly positive, the drinking that went with it, was not.

By now alcohol was definitely starting to make its appearance known in the way I looked and felt. I was drinking daily, now, and it had increased. When I looked in the mirror my hair often looked lank, even though it was newly washed, and my eyes sunken. My skin was not great, and my teeth were often stained. Thread veins started to appear around my nose, cheeks, and on my legs. And my memory was gradually getting worse. I had started to lose chunks of my past memories as well. But most of it was while Daniel was poorly, so I assumed it was another clever coping mechanism.

Something, I am not sure what, started to trigger little warning signs in my head. My thoughts would drift to little lurches of worry. Was I damaging my health with the amount I was drinking? It was far beyond the so-called government guidelines. I started to get adverts on my social feed for liver function tests, so I bought one, and was relieved when my level was still in the green. It was high though… so I bought another few over the next couple of years, just to keep an eye on things. They definitely weren't cheap!

Financially, alcohol was starting to play a part in pushing us into debt. By now my husband had started drinking too. We were already in trouble - having a child with challenging health conditions is incredibly costly, and we had to sell a lot of things to keep paying the bills. I was still working with Steve, and we were both self employed. I knew we would probably not be able to maintain the lifestyle we were enjoying for much longer without one of us going back to full time employment. And as I had the experience in the corporate workplace, that someone would have to be me.

Additionally, I had started to drink to excess at nights. Usually, this was fine and I would just go to bed and sleep it all off. But occasionally I would browse the Internet, and buy things, which was further costing us. Once, I even bought a Jack Vettriano painting - my favourite artist, with a very large credit card payment. I had to call them the following morning to cancel it. I was mortified at the time! I would have loved that painting even to this day. But it would have definitely thrown us under the bus for the mortgage payments, that's for sure.

On top of everything, my wine purchases got more and more expensive, as I had decided, somehow, that the better quality the wine, the healthier it would be for me. Not only was I buying vegan wine, and organic wine, but I was trying to spend a "good" amount on wine to make sure I was not putting "rubbish" into my body. Can you believe that? Bonkers. I studied which wines were good, and thought I was a bit of a wine aficionado at one point. I read books on the subject, learning about all the different types of grape and the type of grape each vineyard specialised in. Madness, really, when you consider it was all just ethanol, plain and simple, be it four pounds a bottle, or forty.

And have you ever shopped in a supermarket for wine, and only bought wine? The "halo" purchases of unhealthy food, and random things like air fryers, that went into my basket as I shopped, could have filled a two bedroom house over the years. I was too embarrassed to just buy wine. I thought it would expose me as an alcoholic. So I added lots of other things to my basket to feel safer about going to the checkout. More money down the drain on things I did not need. Only to then be ashamed again when I had to take all the bottles to the bottle bank to recycle them. How I hated all those bags full of bottles. I used to be at the bottle bank for ages. I was scared the neighbours would recognise me. The self-loathing was awful.

Added to the health and financial woes alcohol gave me, was awful sleep deprivation. Did you know that when you drink to excess, you are not getting any good sleep at all? No REM sleep, your body basically shuts down all your systems so it can deal with the poison you have just imbibed. Simple. And if you wake up after a heavy bout of drinking, having passed out earlier, it was your body shutting you down because it could no longer keep you functioning, the amount of poison was so much. How scary a thought is that? Terrifying.

I would wake up at 2am, 3am, 4am, worrying about everything, And worrying about what I might have said or done while I was drinking. And worrying about money, and the fact I might have to go back to working for the corporate world. I would check my phone and my socials in case I had added anything silly, frequently. And I would dread the pictures the following day, after a night out, because I knew I would look like a twerp. Or I would creep down the stairs, checking everyone's faces in case I had been a jerk to them the previous night, and then breathe a sigh of relief when they all seemed to still like me.

And if I had said something horrible, and nobody was speaking to me, I would have to try and find out what it was I had said. I would listen for clues as to what the fight may have been about, and even felt relief when my husband started the fight again, because at least then I knew what I had done! On occasion, I would even just apologise without actually knowing what it was I was apologising for, or even whether it was my fault. It probably was my fault, but is that any way to live? Creeping around your life, worrying what you have said, or done, or acted like? It was a nightmare I will never, ever miss.

There were also bruises - huge black bruises, and mystery cuts. I would occasionally, when feeling brave, show Steve, and he would tell me he had heard crashing in the bathroom, perhaps, or that he had found me legs akimbo in the bath. Or I had slipped up the stairs on my way to clean my teeth. Part of me was just glad I was still remembering to clean my teeth, the other part of me was mentally rubbing my sore shins, and promising not to drink as much that night, and to stop being an idiot with alcohol. But as 7pm approached, my brain would tell me it was time for my nightly glass of wine. Or seven.

"I'll just have one glass tonight", I'd silently say to myself, feeling an enormous surge of relief as the corkscrew entered the cork in the bottle, and started its journey winding into the cork to aid its eventual release. As I lifted the cork from the neck of the bottle, the aroma of the wine filled me with satisfaction, and I loved the sound of it slugging into my latest designer wine glass, resplendent in its refinery of roses pained up the side of it, or gold flecks and little diamanté embellishments. Sometimes I would leave the wine in the kitchen, to return to it as I finished each glass, but if I was playing a game, or watching a movie, I would bring both the glass and the bottle with me, carefully resting both on the little table beside me. The first sip would give me great satisfaction. I would promise myself - only two glasses tonight, or only three glasses tonight, not knowing that the only glass you really need to refuse yourself, is the first.

And then there was the damage to my relationships. As I was drinking at home, I could not jump in the car and drive to friends' houses, or go out, so some of my friendships dried up. And the relationship between my husband and I became more and more distanced. He smoked, and would sit outside in the garden for most of the evening, watching the bats fly around. Whereas I preferred to drink in the warmth and safety of my living room. I would either play games or watch TV. Our lives slowly drifted apart. I believe we came close to splitting up, like so many other couples who have lost a child. I have no idea how we held it together. We were the only couple out of all of those we had met, whose marriage remained intact. But it certainly wasn't through effort on my part. Or his. We were both too broken.

And, worst thing yet, was how grumpy I would be in the morning for the school runs or for work. Head banging with hangovers, and then, as my body became used to the nightly drinking, grumpiness replaced headaches and hangovers. I would bash around crossly when getting ready in the mornings, grumbling that I had to be up and about so early. I could never see the beauty in things, as I do now I am free from alcohol. I would march Levi to school, and march back home to work, before jumping on my game for a bit to spend some time with my online friends. By now the wine had worn off, and I was back to being a functioning human being, at least until 7pm came, where I would repeat the cycle again. Just reading this back makes me depressed. I want to reach out to her and give her a hug, and tell her it will be okay.

And so, that is how I fell into the alcohol trap.

Now I am going to show you the way to get back out.

There is science behind the reasons for all of this, and I'll cover that very briefly next. It's not boring, I promise! Actually, its all about you, and your clever, clever human brain…

CHAPTER FOUR

Why alcohol helps, and why it hinders, during a life-changing event

"Don't let the bastards grind you down."

— Margaret Atwood

How Alcohol can help us during bad times

Picture this: A black and white movie. The guy has just been dumped by his beautiful wife, and thrown out of the house. So he heads for the nearest bar, and nurses a lowball glass of neat whisky in his hand. He is staring into space. He takes a dramatic swig, finishing the contents of the glass in one gulp, and sets the glass firmly back on the bar.

"Another shot, bar keeper. And leave me the bottle."

It really is no surprise that we turn to alcohol in times of need, is it, when we have grown up surrounded by the stuff?

Watch anything on TV and it almost beggars belief how much alcohol features in every single movie. It could be a too-much-booze-swigging heroine in a romantic comedy. Or perhaps it's an alien with an elongated head, serving purple cocktails to a bounty hunter in the latest Sci-Fi offering. Alcohol has its place everywhere in movie-land, it would seem.

Another issue is alcohol is cheap. In fact, it's probably cheaper right now than it has ever been. Alcohol Change UK say: "From 2009 to 2019, the price of alcohol decreased by 5% relative to retail prices and became 13% more affordable than in 2008. Alcohol is 74% more affordable than it was in 1987."

And marketers have come up with a million ways of making it more palatable now, too, mainly with the addition of bright colourings and lots of sugar to mask the previously nasty taste. Nowadays, if you want to lose yourself in a bottle of something, it's really easy to find your poison, and it isn't going to cost you a lot.

The three most stressful things in your life, according to studies, are:

1. Death of a loved one.
2. Divorce.
3. Moving house.

If you have just lost a loved one, you are not only faced with the most stressful thing in your life, you are also potentially faced with at least one of the other two as well, particularly if you lose a child or partner.

My friend, you can hardly be blamed for heading into oblivion via the bottle. And even if you were not deliberately heading there, the addictive nature of alcohol, coupled with the fact it now has a job to do in your life, will certainly pull you down there pretty quickly.

If you are in the UK, a message on every bottle demands that you: "Drink responsibly!"

Erm, okay, but it's a poisonous substance that is harmful to my health. The World Health Organisation agrees that there is no safe limit for alcohol. They have proven that alcohol is a known carcinogen. So, err, just how are we supposed to drink responsibly? The message appears to blame the imbiber if they drink too much. Is that right? I think not.

Back in the day, alcohol was used by surgeons carrying out operations to numb their patients before cutting into them, or to remove limbs. It was very effective at knocking patients out. However, they had to stop using it, because the amount required for the operation killed far too many patients. New methods were found, and now surgeons have much safer methods of anaesthetising a patient. Phew!

So, alcohol does numb the world of pain you are feeling. And, for a time, that certainly feels nice. I was even able to smile and laugh again when I was tipsy, especially at work events.

And then there is the buzz of alcohol, that can feel nice, can't it?

Except it lasts for around twenty minutes. Yep - That's it. Twenty minutes.

Maybe you just paid £7 for a quick 20 minute buzz. If you drink a lot, you might not even get 20 minutes. And then you spend another £7 on another 20 minutes, except this time it does not last as long. It is not quite so intense. So you are now spending a lot more than £7 to drink more and more, chasing that initial buzz.

Don't believe me? Drink mindfully, with a journal in front of you, and set a timer. The results will blow your mind.

You then fall into a fitful sleep, with no REM activity, which is not proper sleep at all. Certainly not the sleep you need to cope with the grief and anxiety you are having to deal with, and all the demands on your time if you are looking after someone who is sick. So you toss and turn, or wake up at 2am in a ball of fear and anxiety, and things run through your head all night. And then the mean voice in your head starts: "Ugh, idiot! Why did you have to drink so much again? Never again! I need to stop this." The voice is never kind.

Of course, alcohol solves nothing, so when you wake up the following day, often with a hangover, your problems are still there. Added to that, you now have increased anxiety and depression caused by the crash in dopamine, so you mood-swing for the next few days as you adjust, fighting off those awful feelings...

Or, of course, you could drink again? That will get rid of this hangover, or at least push the issue down the road a little. Hmm, which to choose, which to choose...?

Invariably, because alcohol is addictive, you drink again to chase the old feeling. And off you go again. The cycle is never ending.

Still think numbing yourself helps? Still thinking alcohol helps?

How alcohol can hinder

The work required for the body to rid itself of all that ethanol is enormous, and it is dangerous work. Alcohol stays in your system for a long time, and while your body works on ways to rid itself of the poison you just ingested, it only focuses on this, and pauses all other essential maintenance work. If you are lucky, it will eject the poison from your system the quick way, and force it up and out of you, hopefully into the toilet bowl. But often not, when you cannot make it to the bathroom quickly enough. If you are unlucky, your body will now spend days trying to flush the poisons out of your system.

Alcohol affects every part of your body. The biggest thing it affects is your brain.

Sure, all that extra artificially boosted dopamine felt great last night, but now it has been replaced with the after effects of dopamine leaving your system… Your mood will sink, you might feel dehydrated, dizzy, confused about simple things, or as if your head and body are disconnected. It is not nice. And if we keep drinking, our body might stop making dopamine, thinking we do not need it, which can cause depression and low mood.

Crumbs, if you are grieving, you really do not need that.

Anxiety can increase as you lose both of the artificial dopamine and serotonin boosts it gained from alcohol, which are our happy hormones. Hey - we need that! Long-term use can cause actual shrinkage of the brain, as well.

Scary stuff. And that is without even looking at the damage it could do to our bodies.

If you are feeling low or anxious as a result of a post-drinking session crash, you will be unable to be present for anyone, including yourself. "Great!" You might argue, "I do not want to be present right now!" But you need to move through grief, the *only* way is through, and hiding from it not only prolongs the pain and suffering for you, it also prolongs it for everyone else involved.

Your brain will remember the temporary, artificial dopamine and serotonin high alcohol gave you, and it will demand more, and you might not be in a good position to fight off the cravings, leading to a risk that you start using alcohol to lower anxiety. It will work, temporarily, but the following morning you will crash even harder, and this leads to a horrible cycle. It can even lead to other serious mental health issues, and several physical issues, or illness.

They don't write any of that on the bottle, do they?

Becoming alcohol dependent can leave you in a quandary as you begin to drop other healthy habits, too, all of which are extremely important as you move through the grieving process. You might forget to go out, or not want to go out. You might skip exercise altogether, especially when you are hungover, and spend the day in front of the TV instead, and a hangover-recovering body can sometimes be hard to move. There were plenty of days slouching on the sofa for me, flicking through Netflix, instead of going out in the sunshine, or exercising, or doing anything. Hell, on some days I did not even get out of bed until 2pm.

Perhaps you do not eat well, either, preferring things that are quick to grab, such as junk food, or sweet things, or fatty fry-ups. Who wants to grate fresh coleslaw when they are dealing with the hangover from hell? Ooh… who left this family pack of Cheetos in the cupboard? And chocolate… mmmm. That's lunch sorted, then!

Then there are the darker sides of alcohol dependance, including a loss of inhibitions, increased crime rates, and sickness. Here are some facts from Alcohol Change UK:

- In 2015/16 in England, victims believed the offender(s) to be under the influence of alcohol in 39% of all violent incidents.
- Alcohol is a causal factor in more than 60 medical conditions, including: mouth, throat, stomach, liver and breast cancers; high blood pressure, cirrhosis of the liver; and depression.
- Alcohol misuse is the biggest risk factor for death, ill-health and disability among 15-49 year-olds in the UK, and the fifth biggest risk factor across all ages.
- In 2020, in the UK, the alcohol-specific death rate was 14 per 100,000 people, an 18.6% increase compared with 2019 and the highest increase since the records began.

[More facts & statistics on alcohol can be found on this brilliant site: Alcohol Change UK – https://alcoholchange.org.uk/alcohol-facts/fact-sheets/alcohol-statistics]

Sobering stuff, if you'll excuse the pun.

And, finally, your loved ones will begin to lose you, as you disappear into alcohol dependance, and they will worry about you. Worry you are not healing, which, of course, you are not. You are merely shunting your grief and pain into the next day. I shunted mine for almost a decade before I started dealing with it.

Now for the good news

Okay, so that was depressing. There is some good news here though. For example:

1. You do **not** have to have a problem with alcohol, in order to decide to take a break, or give it up altogether.

2. You do **not** have to hit rock bottom before you pull up and out of alcohol dependance.

3. You are living in a time where the medical science on alcohol dependence is better than it has ever been, so you have more support options than ever before, if you choose to take advantage of them.

4. Where deciding not to drink alcohol anymore used to be a big decision often questioned by friends and family, it is now becoming more and more common to do so, even if it is just for health reasons.

5. Grieving is far, far easier without alcohol, and you will move all the way through it much faster if you go through it naturally.

6. You have the power to change your habits! And it does not take as long as you might think. You simply need to change your mindset from alcohol helping you, to alcohol hindering you. What you do not want, you will never crave.

7. Your brain is an awesome piece of kit! The habits you no longer have need of will dissipate, like a grown over pathway in the forest which is no longer used, because you made a new pathway. When I learned of this in my coach training, it blew my mind!

8. Your lasting memories of your loved one will be sweeter and more positive without alcohol.

During my training at This Naked Mind Institute, I learned that there are four stages of alcohol dependance that we must move through in order to achieve freedom. As someone who is grieving, this also offers us peace and expediency through the grieving process. This was beyond helpful to me, and now I want to share it with you. It is my hope that knowing this information shortens the time you spend within the painful process of moving on from losing a loved one.

The stages are:

1. Asleep - Unaware of the issue, unaware of the need to change.
2. Aware - Aware of the issue, unsure how to change.
3. Awake - Aware of the issue, you know how to change.
4. Alive - Completely free of the issue, no need to change.

You are in the right place. I have been where you are. Now let's see if we can bring you closer to stage four. Note: Some things will be repeated, but this is because they are important.

Read on, my friend. There is a huge amount of hope here for you in the pages that follow.

CHAPTER FIVE

Understanding what alcohol does to numb you

"You have brains in your head. You have feet in your shoes.
You can steer yourself any direction you choose.
You're on your own. And you know what you know.
And YOU are the one who'll decide where to go... "

— Dr. Seuss - Oh, the Places You'll Go! HarperCollins, 2011.

Losing years to alcohol dependance - From Asleep to Aware

Almost nine years passed with no change for me. I was unaware of any issue, to be honest. During the day I was fairly high functioning. During the night, I was a gamer who drank 'the government weekly safe amount' every single night. I was still healthy, luckily, and had no real issues about my activities, although friends later said how worried they were for me. My mental state of the problem, was "asleep". I was unconscious of the fact any change was needed. Any awareness that alcohol might not be doing me any good was firmly buried in my subconscious.

And then, a couple of little things happened that jolted me into the next stage of mental awareness. This meant I was suddenly conscious that I probably needed to change my ways, but I had no idea how.

Firstly, our finances had been very slowly trickling away ever since Daniel had passed away. Having a child with serious health issues is ridiculously expensive, with travel and time off work, and all the costs of eating and drinking while you are away. We were both self-employed and each of us earning a decent income, there was very little state help for us available. However our employment status also covered up the fact we were slowly losing revenue, and my drinking probably did not help with the management of our finances either. Every year my husband was getting worse, mentally and physically, so his business suffered badly. I realised we might not be able to pay our bills. We could even lose our home.

With me on a sturdier road to recovery than Steve, who was still angry about the loss of his eldest son, it would be me who had to take action. This, of course, meant I would need to go back to the corporate world, and get a full-time job, I realised with dismay. I had not really been out of the house for years, other than the odd outing with my best friend into town, so this realisation was terrifying. It was also the end to my dream of being my own boss. I loved being my own boss so much.

I knew I needed to acclimatise, so I joined a Tai Chi class at the local gym, in order to gently bring myself back into the real word. There I met a legion of lovely retirees, all of whom asked nieces and nephews and grandkids about roles for computer geeks who had been out of the employment market for a while. I even learned a little Tai Chi! They were an amazing bunch of people, and a few were ex-businessmen and Naval officers who had achieved seniority during their careers. They gave me lots of good advice, for which I will be forever grateful.

Feeling a little more confident, I put my CV onto an online job search engine.

Within two hours, I received a call from an agency with something that sounded like a job I could do. Within 24 hours I had been interviewed and offered the job. I had not even been able to drive back home! It was there I would stay for the next 15 years of my career.

At first it was a fabulous place to be. I was completely anonymous, and I was no longer "Cancer Mum". Nobody knew my history, nobody shot me any looks of pity, or sympathy. I never once heard the phrase "there but for the grace of God go I", which was something I overheard frequently at the school gates.

The work was pretty easy, and everyone just assumed I had taken a career break to have kids, so no questions were asked. I joined a few groups at work, and even joined a weight loss group in the evenings, and I think I started to heal pretty well.

I did well at work, earning myself a few promotions, and making a few new friends. And when I got home I was able to jump on the game I loved so much. Even Steve seemed to cheer up a little now the responsibility for the finances was no longer fully on his shoulders. It looked like everything might be okay!

Except, you guessed it, I was still drinking nightly. Externally I would laugh heartily, and I socialised with my colleagues with big, bright smiles and a happy hello in the morning.

But when I got home I disappeared into a pretty dark place. I still missed Daniel, and I had by now had another son, a new brother for Levi. I was tired, and spent, and yes, still pushing the grieving journey further and further into myself, instead of dealing with anything. When work was good, I would be okay, but if things started to go wrong at work, which of course was often in a corporate setting full of politics and sales, I would drown my sorrows hard into the night with a glass of wine, or six. It wasn't ideal, and it went on for a further ten years. But I functioned okay, and I was good at my job, so, like many others in my position, I coped and I carried on.

Being aware of an issue, but not knowing what to actually do about it, is one of the most painful places to be in, because you feel trapped. It is often a place where people most need the help of a coach or a therapist to get unstuck, but somehow, I got myself out on my own. But it took far too long, and I wish now I had found the help I needed and shortened the time wasted being stuck. Almost two decades in the same place. It does not bare thinking about, and one could argue it took all of my prime years.

If I can stop you being there for so long, my friend, then my job here will be done.

Aware to Awake - Waking up to the issue

"Awakening" to your drinking means by now you are fully conscious you might be drinking too much, and you are now capable of fixing it.

And this is often where you will be left when you seek help from other sources. If you go into rehab, or join Alcoholics Anonymous, they will all be satisfied that you are no longer drinking. However, this is not the end of the journey, not by any means, and my next story will tell you why.

It was 2018, and by now I was fully awake to the issue I had with alcohol. I had put on weight, and I was struggling to lose it because I was drinking too many calories in the wine I was consuming. Also, a friend at my slimming group had just catapulted herself to target weight, after years of being stuck, simply because she gave up alcohol. She was my drinking buddy, the one who laughed with me at the fact we were saving up food calories for gin and wine at the weekends. She was a complete hoot, but she was getting frustrated at paying five pounds a week and not getting anywhere on her weight loss journey. So, suddenly, she just stopped drinking!

I was so pleased for her as I applauded her getting to target, and took pictures for our Facebook Group as she was having the "Slimmer of the Month" sash draped over her. She looked stunning - maybe ten years younger! Witnessing her journey to success was one of the first big signals to my brain that alcohol might not be doing me any good. I had to get it back under control.

So I bought a few books on giving up alcohol, and took a 30 day challenge for charity, to see if I could take a break.

I lasted around ten days before jumping back to the safety of my wine every evening. I paid the charity all the money though, and I told everyone I had succeeded in quitting for 30 days. I was lying to myself as well as lying to everyone else. The experience troubled me greatly, but it had indicated to me that I might have an issue.

Feeling determined, I took on another challenge, this time with a 30 day video challenge. Learning the science side of things was great for my cognitive understanding of exactly what alcohol was doing to me. It worried me, learning about all the harm it did, and I sent for the first of many liver tests through an online company. When it came back, it was just inside the green zone, and I breathed a sigh of relief.

I also had a few outward signs that alcohol was affecting my health. I was often forgetful, and I sometimes found it harder to do things I had once found really easy. My eyesight had started to suffer too. My GP said my blood pressure was too high, which was a big shock, because previously it had always been too low. My ankles started to get puffy, and my face looked puffy too, especially after a heavy night of drinking. And I had started to look forward to Fridays, because it meant I could drink without worrying about driving the following morning. Meaning I could drink a lot more. Something had to change, and I knew that thing was alcohol.

For the next few years I toyed with various alcohol breaks, doing courses, and challenges for charity, none of which lasted long, but each time I seemed to be able to stay away for longer and longer. It was a lot of stop-starts, all of which caused a huge amount of stress and upset because I felt that I had failed each time. But by now I had the motivation to keep going, and each time I read something new, it would chip away at my thoughts and beliefs about alcohol, challenging them, and stripping them away.

I was now fully awake, and I understood alcohol was not only harming me, it had never helped me in the first place. A huge shift happened to me internally when I read Annie Grace's book for the second time, the brilliant This Naked Mind, and around this time Annie also launched a mini course as well. I joined up readily. Sadly, at the very same time, perimenopause hit me like a lump hammer, and my emotions started to spike all over the place, causing me all sorts of upset and emotional turbulence. This, coupled with bullying incidents at work, sent me hurtling backwards, emotionally. Somehow, I have no idea how, I held on to the alcohol freedom I had found. I just cried a lot instead.

I did not know it back then, but the shift inside me had started to move me to a fourth stage: Alive.

Awake to Alive - Becoming Alive

In creating this book, I left this part as the very last part I would write to you, my friend, because it was the bit I was most looking forward to writing.

As I said previously, most traditional alcohol therapies, rehabs and even Alcoholics Anonymous, stop treatment once a person reaches the "Awake" stage, above. They treat the behaviour, not the emotions and beliefs around alcohol, so the person is often left white-knuckling it, and thinking they would be stuck in alcohol-free boredom for the rest of their lives. That they were an addict, pure and simple, not normal, and they would never be allowed to touch a drop of alcohol, ever again. Often these plans blame the drinker. Not the substance. If they "fall off the wagon" it is their fault, and they can lose their membership.

That is a painful place to be for anyone. But if you have lost someone meaningful in your life, and you are still grieving, you will wonder what the hell you might have done to deserve to be stuck like this. All you were doing was using the wrong tool. But it was the easiest, and most socially acceptable tool available to you at the time. You were not aware it was the wrong tool at the beginning. You did not even know alcohol was an addictive substance! I certainly didn't! Why on earth is it legal to advertise an addictive drug? None of us really stood a chance.

So, before going on with my story, let me clear a few things up. It's important.

1. None of this is your fault. None of it.

2. You were simply using the wrong tool. It was readily available, and it shouldn't have been. It is one of my greatest hopes that alcohol will soon be treated in the same manner as cigarettes. Then it will no longer be socially acceptable to drive alcohol down our, or our kids, throats all the time on TV and on billboards and in bars.

3. Every human being is susceptible to becoming dependable on alcohol. Everyone. It is addictive. It is a drug. It kills more people globally, every year, than all the illegal drugs and smoking put together. It is the worst drug of all.

4. There was never any way you were able to "Drink Responsibly." You were doomed from the start. It is not on the person to control it. The way in which alcohol works is insidious. And drinking alcohol being socially acceptable, and almost expected of you, makes it more so.

5. Within your drink is a few drops of ethanol. That is all alcohol is. Ethanol. The only thing ethanol is good for, is a car. It is the same ethanol as in petrol. Oh, and it makes a great hand sanitiser or kitchen cleaner. Those few drops of ethanol are what you are resting all your hopes on. For peace from grief, enjoyment on a night out, or a fun holiday. You are giving those few drops of ethanol far too much importance in your life. Unless you love driving a petrol car, in which case, carry on. I have always wanted a Mustang, myself. One day, eh?

6. I am going to say it again, so it goes into your brain… **None of this is your fault.**

Okay, with that done, I shall move on with my story.

As I said, I knew nothing about the various stages of addiction back then, but I had now moved into the "Alive" stage, the fourth and final stage of recovery with This Naked Mind methodology. It took around a month after I had stopped drinking, and then a further few months with no alcohol, when the wonderful benefits of being alcohol free started to amplify.

The difference, my friend, was astounding! It was almost as if a huge weight had been lifted off me, allowing me to see the world as I used to, before I started drinking. And my gosh, that world was bright, and so beautiful!

Work was still rubbish sometimes, but I found myself far better geared to deal with it. I simply looked forward to going home again on a stressful day. I looked forward to seeing my family and friends, my support network, instead of opening a bottle of wine.

In the mornings I would wake up so much happier, and I appreciated the birds singing, or the sunshine, or the rain pattering on my bedroom window - all the little things. It sounds corny, but I think a big part of the joy I felt was in not having to worry about how much I had drunk the previous night, or who I had upset. Lifting that stress and pain away was so beneficial to me. No more worrying about headaches and shooting pains in my chest, wondering if it was something more dangerous than a hangover.

My sleep had improved tenfold, and I was dreaming so well. I actually looked forward to going to bed to sleep. It felt as though I had gone back to when I was a child, when I absolutely adored sleep. And I felt clear headed and bright after a good nights sleep. My brain was sharper.

My appearance had improved massively, I looked less bloated and puffy, and my eyes were brighter.

But the most remarkable thing of all was the improvement in my mental state.

When I was drinking every night I was anxious and probably very depressed. Now I felt brighter and better able to deal with life's little woes. Many of the health issues and anxiety issues I had previously blamed on the perimenopause simply disappeared. Not all of them, mind, but we will come to that later.

My job was pretty technical, and despite several updates to the technology I was easily able to learn the new systems and keep up with all of the fast-paced movement in the digital world. I do wonder how possible that might have been if I was still lost in the fog of daily drinking.

Newly invigorated, but determined to speed up my progress, I hired a life coach who specialised in the menopause. She showed me tactics for better nutrition and practices that would lower my issues with perimenopause. She was my staunch supporter right when I needed it. I will be forever grateful to her. She praised my progress, and I moved onwards into my new state of mind, happy and alcohol free.

My GP was also pleased with my results, although I do not think she quite believed me when I said I was alcohol free. She allowed me the HRT patches I had been fighting to get for so long, because in lowering alcohol consumption I had vastly reduced my risk of breast cancer. And with my new patches, I also lost all the hot flashes, night sweats and rollercoaster emotions I had been going through while I was still drinking.

Suddenly feeling like I could take on any mountain, I decided to retrain myself to help others out of the alcohol trap. I wanted to share this amazing new knowledge with the world. So, I bit the bullet, and got a loan from my bank to pay for training as an Alcohol Freedom Coach with the *This Naked Mind* Institute. It felt right, because it was the biggest lever that helped me to get out of my own troubles with alcohol. I also loved the non-judgmental approach and compassionate methods.

The course was long, intense and super hard to follow sometimes, but I studied hard. I practiced coaching every night, and worked for my corporate job all day. It was probably the most intense thing I have ever taken on in my life. But the people I met were wonderful, incredible like-minded individuals, all of whom had travelled their own journeys with alcohol. We all soon became fast friends.

We met up on Zoom calls regularly, and coached each other on absolutely everything, honing our new skills. I occasionally helped them with digital marketing where I could, or by giving advice on websites. I had found a wonderful world, and for the first time in over a decade, I felt like I fit in perfectly. I had finally found my tribe.

As we neared the end of the course, I dreamed of all the people I would be able to help. We all did. It was so empowering. And even though I was working hard, the work was energy-giving. I knew I had found the right place to take the next step into my new life.

And the biggest shift of all, for me, was that I no longer cared about alcohol. It was so small and insignificant to me. It meant nothing to me. It still means nothing. I would as much want to drink alcohol now, as I would the bleach I keep under my kitchen sink.

Imagine feeling like that. Imagine a future you, where you no longer have to care about alcohol at all, where it doesn't even enter your thoughts!

How does it feel? I hope it feels good, because now it's my goal in life, to help people get to that place.

And all I needed to do, in order to find myself, and this wonderful, incredible life, was give up wine. Just wine.

Next, I have a rather clever "future you" exercise that really worked for me when I figured out I was in trouble with alcohol. I think it might help you, too. Read on, my friend!

CHAPTER SIX

Versions of You

"How wonderful it is that nobody need wait a single moment before starting to improve the world."

—Anne Frank

Do you remember a movie called Sliding Doors? I loved that film, I like anything time travel or alternate reality based. Or sci-fi. I'm a massive geek for these things.

In case you have not seen it, it was a "what-if" scenario in which a character called Helen, played by Gwyneth Paltrow, is fired from her job in PR. In one scenario she misses her subway train, and in the other she catches it. Then the movie shows the two versions of her life play out, and you get to decide which one is heading in the right direction. It's a great film - definitely worth a watch.

Quick question… What if I told you you could star in your own version of Sliding Doors, right now?

Hear me out here. I'm deadly serious. Let's take a look at how it might pan out…

Take 1: You, version one.

Ok, so in scenario number one, you drank last night. It's a Friday, its cool, but you woke up at 2am, heart pounding, wishing you hadn't drunk so much. Or anything at all for that matter. You tossed and turned for a bit. Then you got worried about that nagging shooting pain in your chest that keeps coming back, and you wonder if alcohol might be damaging your health. You need to send off for that liver test soon, and maybe get your blood pressure checked.

What ensues next is a lot of nighttime worrying and turning things over in your head, wondering if you have given yourself heart disease with all the prolonged drinking, or cancer, or worse. In fact, you have been having headaches for a while now… and your old friend from school… Didn't she die really young from alcohol-induced reasons? Your heart starts pounding, and you cannot stop thinking about all the little things that have been wrong with you for ages now. Ugh - WHY do you keep doing this to yourself? Why can't you just drink normally? After a couple of hours of tossing and turning, feeling anxious and with several concerning thought-streams running through your head, you eventually fall into a fitful sleep again.

You wake up later than planned, and wince at the headache you now have. Your head feels blurry. Stumbling out of bed, you drag yourself to the bathroom to clean your teeth, and grimace at what beholds you in the bathroom mirror. Perhaps you have make up down your face because you did not wash it off last night before passing out in your bed. Or maybe you have a light bruise below your eye, and you cannot remember for the life of you how you might have procured it.

Your eyes look sunken and dark, and is that a yellow tinge in them? No, you are seeing things. Mental note to self: You really need to get that liver function test sorted out.

At least you had a good night, you think to yourself. But then you look at yourself in the mirror and screw up your nose. Hmmm... What DID happen last night? Not knowing makes you feel unsettled. You remember the start of the event. You remember buying a few rounds of drinks. And then someone brought the sweet, sickly shots out. Despite hating them, you drink at least four. After that memories of the night go fuzzy. How did you get home last night? And with who?

Your heart lurches a little at not being able to remember the previous night. You scrabble back to your bedroom and search for your phone. Opening it with shaking hands, you quickly scroll through your socials. Did you write anything on them last night? Were there any clues as to what happened? You feel nauseous and you drop the phone onto your bed and hastily run back to the bathroom, only just making it to the toilet before throwing up disgusting green vomit laced with some sort of greasy food residue. Gross! However, once your stomach has emptied itself of last night's shenanigans you do feel moderately better.

You cook up a greasy breakfast of eggs, bacon and sausage to try and soak up some of last nights alcohol. Hell, you even throw a piece of bread into the frying pan. Nothing like fried bread to help with hangovers. The smell of greasy food makes you feel a little queasy again, but you are not sick this time. You just have a killer headache, for which you grab a couple of aspirin and take them with a glass of water. Rooting around in your cupboards, looking for the new prescription your GP gave you last week, you think about last night again. It annoys you that you cannot remember what happened. Having found them at last, you take a couple of the anti-anxiety pills you got from your doctor, then slam the cupboard shut, wincing at the noise level slightly. Then you reach for the first of the seven coffees you will have this morning. You will need them to start to feel like you again.

Full of a fry-up, you switch on the TV, and settle in front of a box drama set you will never remember, and loaf on the sofa until it starts to get dark outside again. You know you should be tidying up the house, or getting some of your studying done, but you just cannot be bothered. Or perhaps you fire up a game, and play it deep into the evening. You call this "you time", but honestly, the way you feel, you can barely do anything else. You need to self heal, you think to yourself, and try to recover. A small part of you feels guilty for wasting a whole Saturday doing nothing, especially when it is so sunny and beautiful outside. You were supposed to be going to a bar with your Mum, but you do not feel up to it. She will understand, you suppose, as you flip through channels randomly, not finding a single thing to watch.

As the evening draws in to a close you pick up your mobile phone and start scrolling through socials to see what other people are up to. You are disappointed to see your brother and your Mum are at the local bar. You so wanted to go to that, you are gutted. You had all been talking about it for weeks. Your brother was playing in his band, on stage, for the first time ever. You half wish you had not gone out last night. Was it even worth it? Who knows! You don't even remember, and you just threw up £100 worth of alcohol into the toilet, you think to yourself glumly.

Your heart almost stops in your chest as you start seeing your friends' pictures from last night. You do NOT look good... Oh, no! How horrifically embarrassing. You look like a proper idiot! How in hell's name did you get into that sort of position! No wonder nobody has been in touch today. You tentatively feel around your knee area, and sure enough, there is bruising all around it and slight swelling. Hooking up your pyjamas you check it. It's almost completely black and purple. Worryingly so. Ugh!

Flipping to messages, you see you have missed seven messages from your best mate, wanting to know where you are and whether you got home safely. Hastily you text back - you're fine, you reply. For the next hour you message each other back and forth, and your heart sinks again as the night becomes clearer through the tales she tells you. None of it jogs any memories, but you do get snippets of images every now and again, so you are fairly sure this is all true.

It turns out last night you had gotten yourself into a pointless argument, started a fight in the back of the bar, and left the club early. You have no idea how you got home, or when, its all a blur. Apparently you were falling all over the place and picking fights with anyone who looked at you sideways. Oh, and you snogged someone you shouldn't have and then told your partner to make them jealous. He called it quits on you, of course. So you phoned your best mate, absolutely shrieking and wailing at her about how he had wronged you for being so honest with him. She tried hanging up on you three times but you kept calling her back. You feel a little guilty as she had work today, and she is shattered. She does, however, forgive you, but kindly says maybe you need to drink a little less next time?

Heart pounding, you get up for another coffee, you feel so dehydrated today. Should you call your partner... Will they even forgive you? You daren't call them. No way. As you rise, there's that sharp chest pain again, and you remember the worries from last night. You wonder again if drinking is harming your health. The stress of this thought causes you to skip the coffee machine and pour a glass of red wine instead, you know it will make you feel better. Even as you pour the wine, you can feel yourself cheer up. Checking the wine rack confirms you have at least another two bottles. This makes you feel safe. You might as well write off today as done, and get an early night.

But first, wine....

Take 2: You, Version 2

You wake up, its Saturday, stretch, and blink at the early daylight in your room. Last night you dreamt deeply, you feel good, and rested. Your stomach rumbles slightly, and you remember with excitement that a new module in your new course lands this morning. You are training for a career change, and it is beyond exciting. A little shiver of anticipation runs through you, and you fling the covers back to go and get showered and clean your teeth.

In the bathroom mirror you observe your eyes are bright and clear, and your skin looks fantastic at the moment. Your hair is thicker, too, and it probably does not need washing today. Weirdly, your eye lashes are so long now too. You had no idea all the alcohol you were drinking caused eye lashes to stop growing, but hey ho!

You clean your teeth, and note that nowadays they are never stained, like they used to be back when you were drinking. Your lips aren't blotchy with purple red wine stains either, and they are smooth and hydrated. You grin at yourself in the mirror. Why on earth did it take you so long to stop drinking alcohol? You look like an advertisement for change! Chuckling to yourself, you close the bathroom cabinet and give yourself a cheeky wink in the mirror.

You step on the bathroom scales, and note with delight you are still slowly losing a little weight each week. You feel great. Jumping in the shower you scrub yourself with the expensive shower gel you bought yourself as a treat last week. It smells amazing. You can afford to treat yourself more often now you are not wasting all your money on alcohol and smelly kebabs on a Friday night. And the money left in your bank account just keeps rising and rising without spending it all on nights out. You still go out, of course, but without the dehydrating effect of alcohol, you enjoy (and I mean, *really* enjoy) two or three drinks now instead of chugging eight or ten down every night. It saves so much money. Nobody told you about any of this before you took your break from booze. Why on earth would you want to go back? You feel so free.

As you make a deliciously healthy breakfast, you smile again at last night. You had met up with your favourite people, and it was just too funny. Honestly, you cannot believe how much you all laughed! It's a shame Pete ruined the evening slightly by drunkenly picking fights with everyone he saw, but the rest of the evening was just hilarious, and you had all managed to get rid of him eventually. One of your friends said they saw him getting taken away by the police because he couldn't stand up. It was probably for his own good to be honest. You feel so lucky to have such great friends. You all went dancing afterwards and it was like being back in the heyday of clubbing. You met up with a load of other people you knew, and everyone just got on so well. Such a happy night. The whole, brilliant night was just what you needed after a long week at work. And, on the plus side, you have a wonderfully clear head this morning. You grimace as you remember the horrendous hangovers you used to get. Thankfully they are all gone now! What isn't there to love?

After coffee and breakfast you take the dog for a walk in the early autumn sunshine, and natter to occasional dog walkers you meet along the way. You find a nice park bench to sit down for a while, you are in no rush today. Your dog grins at you widely, and bounds off to play with her doggy friends as you absentmindedly gaze at the golden trees in the park, dreaming of your potential new career once your course has finished.

Your best friend texts you to say thank you for the fun night, and sends a funny GIF that makes you chuckle again. You chat on text for a bit, and find out Pete was actually arrested and never made it home.

He spent the night in a police cell and his wife had to go collect him. He was shouting and throwing air punches at one of the police women, so he will be in trouble today. Poor Pete. It is his responsibility though. He has a choice, as we all do. At least he was safe, there are some dodgy people out at night, wanting to take advantage of people in his condition. You make up your mind to text him later and see if he was okay.

Calling the dog over to you, you clip her lead to her collar, and take a slow walk home. Once there, you make yourself a coffee, grab your laptop, and mull over this week's study module.

So exciting... it's marketing week! You will learn how to launch your business, and how best to find the clients you will soon be able to help in the same way you were helped all those years ago. The course is invigorating and super interesting, really good stuff, and it motivates you. You switch your browser over to your website, and create a new blog post, telling the world about all the wonderful things that have happened to you ever since you gave up drinking those insidious few drops of alcohol that had once controlled your days and nights. With delight you notice your traffic is rising steadily, and you even have a new subscriber to your newsletters! It makes you smile uncontrollably, and another shiver of excitement travels down your chest into your stomach. Your business is becoming a real entity, and instead of complaining about working in an office, you are well on your way to a complete redirection in your career. You have never felt so empowered or energised by everything. You feel as though you are finally living.

As you get up to make some lunch, you marvel at how much happier you feel, now that alcohol is not stealing your life away. You have a brand new game downloaded on your PC, and you plan on spending a relaxing few hours playing it, before going out again to see your brother play in a band on stage for the first time ever. He is so excited, and you and your Mum being there means the world to him. You could never let him down. You are excited to see how he does, too. You have listened to his music, and he is *really* good! This is his first live session, but he already has loads more booked. He is even giving up his day job to make a living doing what he loves the most.

You are also excited to see your Mum. She has not been very well of late, and you have both grown closer since her diagnosis. You know you do not have forever with her, so every moment you spend with her is precious. A pang of pain shoots through you as you briefly imagine losing her, but it passes quickly. It's normal to feel like like this, you know this. At least you are there for her now, which is what counts. And this is another new thing to do together, which was your plan from the beginning. So far this year you have been to a ballet recital, an opera, the theatre, visited Stone Henge and watched an open air theatre production in the Lakes. You have loads more planned together too, and you love all these wonderful experiences, as does your Mum. You smile to yourself. You are so lucky to have such an awesome family.

Later that afternoon, you walk into the coffee shop to find your Mum waiting, a happy smile reaching her face as she sees you. One massive hug later, you both make your way to the venue where your brother is playing. You grab an alcohol free beer from the bar, and a small glass of wine for your Mum, and settle down at a table which has been reserved for friends and family. A quick hello to the other band members' families, and the band walks out onto the stage. Your brother wears a sheepish grin when he sees you both, and you swear you can see his eyes tear up a little in gratitude. He will completely deny it later, of course, but Mum sees it too, and you smile to yourself as you continue your applause.

The band is unbelievably good! Not a beat missed, and your brother sings and plays perfectly. Loads of your favourite tracks are covered, and then they do a few of their own, which are just too good. After they have finished the set they lay down their guitars and walk over to the family table.

Your brother gives you a big tight hug, and then your Mum another one, and excitedly tells us that there is someone in the audience looking for people to play at a big London venue. He is not sure who it is, though! You look around the room, and see nothing obvious, but you are so excited for him! Someone drops another alcohol free beer on the table for you, and drinks for the rest of the table, and you all settle down to natter about what is going on in your lives right now. You all laugh at each others' news and jokes. It is such a lovely evening. Perfect.

A kerfuffle at the back of the bar, and out races Neil, the drummer in the band. "We did it!" he cries, and we notice a tall man following him out of the bar area, grinning and holding out his hand for your brother to shake. Clasping your brother's hand tightly, and then pulling him into a congratulatory hug, the tall man laughs as your brother is overwhelmed with excitement and happiness, his eyes sparkling. The two men start talking very quickly.

In that moment, looking around at everyone, there is so much love in your heart. You are filled with overwhelming joy. You got be here, right where you needed to be, witnessing what would soon be the biggest shift in your brother's life. He and his band agree to meet up in London later that week and sign a contract, not with a club, as they first thought, but with a record label… An *actual* record label. Your eyes fill with tears, and you are so glad to have been here on this momentous night. What an experience!

It's late, and you have to leave shortly, so you hug your happy brother tightly and congratulate him again, before grabbing your coat and walking out to the car with your Mum. You can drop her off tonight as you have not been drinking. She is appreciative because she hates climbing into cars with strangers at night when she has to get a taxi.

Within the hour you are cleaning your teeth for bed, and you marvel at how incredible your day has been. In the old days you'd have spent it all on the sofa, getting over one of many hangovers, wasting the day with a rubbish TV boxset drama you will never remember.

Switching off your side light, you snuggle into your soft sheets, and look forward to the day tomorrow with hope and a warm heart.

Take 3: You right now.

If you are still drinking alcohol, this might read like a fairy tale to you. It really, truly does not have to.

"Big Alcohol" - the brands you buy - make a LOT of money, literally by making you ill every night. By poisoning you. And then your body has to get rid of all those toxins, and this makes you sick too. To top it off, you pay them a lot of your hard-earned money to do all of this. It kind of adds injury to insult.

Big alcohol brands spend billions of dollars every year on glamorous adverts which promise the world and give you nothing but worry, anxiety and pain. Just like the tobacco industry before. Nights in the adverts are big and glamorous and everyone is sexy and good looking and laughing, slim and well toned, or dressed in stunning gowns that cling to perfect bodies. They all have perfect teeth and perfect hair, and perfect homes. And none of them ever get drunk.

What they never show is people crouched over the toilet puking up a hundred dollars worth of booze, or falling over coffee tables, snogging someone they would never normally take a second look at, or going home with the wrong person. Sometimes, a very wrong person. They never show you crying uncontrollably at something you thought about while wasted, your face all snotty and bloated. Or falling asleep in the corner of the pub and your friends all laughing at you and taking pictures. Or getting arrested and spending the night in a police cell while you "clean yourself up." Or hitting someone with the car you could have sworn you were sober enough to drive. Or watching your partner walk out of the door with a suitcase because they have had enough of your nasty alcoholic tantrums.

Do you think the reason they do not show these scenes is because they are ashamed of their customers?

Why let them use you like this? Why allow them to steal your presence from your loved ones.

Get mad. Get even. Get out.

There is a happy ending here for you when you are free. Think about it for a minute… Nobody ever regrets not drinking the previous night, do they? Hmmm.

Do you feel sorry for people who do not drink? Well, you shouldn't. Guess what one of the first things people who are truly free from alcohol say? They all say: "I wish I had done it sooner." They definitely do not feel sorry for themselves. They know alcohol does nothing good whatsoever.

If you are thinking about taking a break from drinking, you might be asking, will your life be killer boring? And this is my next topic… read on, my friend, because boy, do I have some exciting news for you!

CHAPTER SEVEN

Events and Socialising without alcohol

"If you know you are on the right track, if you have this inner knowledge, then nobody can turn you off… no matter what they say."

—Barbara McClintock

So, you have decided to make a big change, and live alcohol free for a month or two. Good stuff!

Now let's look at how to make that the easiest decision of your life. Or, at the very least, easier than waking up at 3am wondering if you sent your boss a text telling him that you've quit, along with 15 very long reasons why…

Pubs, work outings and social events.

Again, the number one thing to remember if you are "out out" is this…. You do NOT owe anyone an explanation. Got that? Because it's an important one. You owe them nothing, not one dot.

You will be asked, fairly frequently at first while people get used to the non-drinking version of you, why you are doing this. You will be asked if you have a drinking problem. People are super curious, particularly if you were the last one standing at the bar every night at work events.

Now, if you like, you can have a few reasons stashed up ahead of the event. I have given you a few of mine already. Here are some more - For example:

- Kids are poorly at home so I might be needed.
- I'm on a health drive.
- I want to lose weight.
- I'm on a charity project raising money for cancer research.
- I'm on call at work.

These only tend to last a few times though before curiosity is evoked once again. I used to have no idea why friends and colleagues were so fascinated by it all, but they were.

The bottom line is you owe nobody nothing, and "It just doesn't do me any good anymore." usually closed them down for me. Or, for shock value, "because it killed my brother." But that always made me feel a bit guilty afterwards for making them feel bad. What can I say, they asked me a LOT in the beginning.

Are you ready for the reason they keep asking?

It's because they feel threatened. Yup, it is true. Threatened.

Threatened because they feel they are losing you and the status quo of you being a drinking buddy for them. Humans hate change in something they like doing and their brains rebuke it. They enjoyed old you, and they already miss it.

But most of all, they feel threatened by you because of their own thoughts. The one thing you discover most of all by taking a break from alcohol, is how many of your friends, family and colleagues feel exactly the same as you. They have the same concerns, the same worries, the same discomfort with their choices as you. And you deciding to give alcohol a break will trigger their own fears and worries. Their brains react, want to keep them safe, and before they even think about it they will blurt out the questions and try to reason with you.

"Ah, mate, I'll buy you a drink if you like"; "Oh - you'll be no fun tonight, then" or "Don't drink, don't smoke - What do you do?" (Old 1980s Adam Ant reference there… showing my age!)

My advice to you, when friends tease you for not drinking? Take it with a pinch of salt, and the later in the evening or event it gets, the more you will understand why. They quickly forget, and disappear into their own alcohol cloud. But if you allow them to convince you to buy a drink, you will regret it the following day. Maybe even beyond that. Going back to alcohol is a bit like going back to a bad relationship. If you go back, it is still toxic. And you always remember why you gave it up pretty quickly, too.

Okay, here comes the fun part…

Remember how you worried you would be no fun without alcohol? Well, it's the opposite of what is true! Sure, the first night you go alcohol free you will feel a little strange. But the second time will be ten times easier, and the third will just feel awesome. Trust me on this.

The other thing you will discover is that drunk people are very, very dull. They repeat themselves a LOT. I have been going to social events for years now, without alcohol, I'm an old hat. And I have trained myself to leave around 10pm or 10.30pm, which is around the time your drinking buddies will start to get incredibly boring. Without beer goggles you will witness them all repeating the same thing over and over again, and honking with laughter at the most unfunny things imaginable.

It is occasionally brilliant fun to watch a work acquaintance get himself into a fight and then arrested for drunkenly lunging at one of the bar assistants for spilling his beer (which never actually happened.) But trust me, you'll want to be out of the way by the time that happens. You will be unable to stop people doing daft things. If you like you can take pictures for social media later, especially if they were hard on you for not drinking. No, I thoroughly recommend it's best for everyone if you make a quick and quiet exit.

The best thing is you barely even have to say goodbye to people when you leave. Nobody remembers you leaving, and if you play it clever and make sure you are in a few pictures at the event, even better! Take them yourself too - your pictures will be so much better than theirs. All people will remember is that you were there with them. Nobody ever remembers me leaving even though I often give them a big hug goodbye. They just remember I was there, swigging my alcohol free beer, and they even forget I was not drinking.

Another great tactic is becoming the designated driver. Now, when you were white-knuckling your sobriety last time, it felt awful being the driver, didn't it? But now you are choosing not to drink, its awesome.

You are the hero of the story to everyone! Plus if you are super savvy you'll accept the offer of a fiver from each person to cover "petrol"and you can even make a bit of money out of it. I used to give the cash to one of my kids the following day. They loved that. But everyone gets home safe. It makes you feel pretty awesome.

Finally, another quick mention for alcohol-free alternative drinks... These are absolutely amazing, and every year the selection just gets better and better. I love a nice pale ale, or an alcohol free gin and tonic, but make sure the bar treats them like the alcoholic version.

No unceremoniously plonking a bottle and a glass in front of you! No, you want it made like a proper G&T - the ice, the goldfish bowl glass. Hell, even the slices of cucumber. You are paying almost the same as an alcoholic drink, so you want the same ritual, thank you very much.

And that is how to do evenings out well. I actually enjoy them so much more now that I am alcohol free. I still dance, still honk with laughter, and still adore the company of friends and colleagues. Sure, my first outing felt a little odd, but after that it was just great fun. I cannot wait for you to experience it. Remember to savour every moment. You GET to be sober all night, and enjoy it. You GET to wake up the following morning with no hangover. And you get to be present.

Weddings and other big events

Weddings and other big "life events" are often billed as a big challenge by clients to begin with. But let's ask ourselves why?

First of all, 99% of the time it is not our wedding. It is someone else's celebration. Sure, it might be a family member or close friend, and we might have this epic family where everyone gets together and has a rip-roaringly good time getting drunk together. Wait - is that true though?

Seriously - ask yourself - is that true?

Our perception of reality exists only in our heads, so just because we were having a good time, it does not mean everyone at the last wedding was drinking, or even having as much of a good time as you.

For all you know half the room was completely sober, or maybe they had one glass of wine and that was it. Perhaps other family members think it's a shame Uncle Pete ruined it for poor Sammy by getting arrested and messing up the speeches. Perhaps you had simply forgotten that, or you were too inebriated to recall it.

Going to your first big event feels like a big thing when you decide to quit alcohol or take a break. But succeed and it feels totally awesome the day after, I can tell you. The second big event, just like going to pubs and clubs, is a doddle. And by the third you will barely get quizzed on it. People just accept you aren't drinking, and they seriously do not care.

By the third event your threat level has reduced. You are still great fun to be around, and you are not harping on at them, preaching about the dangers of alcohol, hopefully.

And - actually, that's a great point to jump in here with. No matter how amazing you feel without booze, or how educated you get, please don't walk around telling everyone how bad alcohol is for them. It does nobody any favours with you becoming an anti-alcohol preacher bore. Remember when you first started to wonder if you were drinking a little too much? It probably took you a little while to come to the conclusion you might need to cut back or give it up, didn't it? Allow the same for your friends and family. We are able to control exactly one person in our lives, and that person is you and you alone.

No, people around you no longer see you as a threat, and they have relaxed about the fact you no longer drink, and they are more comfortable with the change.

In fact, some family members, whether secretly or otherwise, will be super proud of you. Some will wonder at your Herculean strength, and others will secretly be thinking they might give it a go too, especially as they are seeing you are still having an awesome time, still wickedly funny, and still going out. Look at you! You are starting to pass on the gift of being alcohol free without even trying!

Remember also, you are looking great! Your hair, skin, teeth are looking better. You are no longer bleary eyed, and no longer being a drunken bore by 10pm. Your stories are interesting, and you are a social butterfly! Okay, so maybe not the last one, but the fact is you look better than you did at the last event. Another great part of not drinking is you tend to leave parties looking as good as you started them, instead of mascara running down your face or bits of kebab in your hair. It's pretty much all win-win this side!

It is also hilariously funny watching Uncle Pete get arrested again, and you have some great shots on your phone for the socials of his stunt with the wedding cake. This one might go viral! Or you can send it to one of the shows for £250. They love a drunk wedding video. Win - win!

The only very mild stumbling block is dancing. But literally nobody is watching you, they are all pretty much blackout drunk on free wine. So, get out there and start! You'll love it! Just throw some shapes until you get comfortable - it takes around ten minutes by my reckoning, and before long you too will be absolutely loving the experience of drink-free dancing! I loved it so much, I now even whack on some clubbing music while I do the housework, and dance myself through that too. Great incremental exercise! I do believe we are on another win here.

Music Concerts

Music concerts are often a big worry for those taking a break from alcohol, too. Especially if you are a big fan of them. But, let's look at these from a different angle, too.

I absolutely love a live music event. It does not have to be anyone well-known, just someone who can sing/ play, and I am as happy as a pig in mud. This all stems from my big drinking days with my best friend, when we would go and see a live band every Wednesday at the local pub, and meet up with our faves. Those nights were fantastic fun, but they were also alcohol laden.

My favourite concerts though, are the Muse concerts. They are huge affairs, set in big arenas, and full of Pink Floyd-esque dancers swinging from lightbulbs and surreal visuals... amazing! My favourite one was at Arsenal football stadium, which was my middle son's first ever gig. He was about 15 and he loved the same sort of music as me, so I figured it was time.

It was my first "sober" gig. And I had an attitude about it.

I had been off drink for a good few months by then, so the excitement was wearing off. I had bought the tickets when I was still drinking.

"Ugh." I thought to myself, as I woke up, "What's the point? I'm not going to enjoy it without having a drink."

We caught the train to London, and nattered on the train as we rode up. Levi was pretty excited, and it was infectious.

"Can we go to Wahacas?" he asked.

"Yup, I guess," I say, thinking of the little restaurant in Soho we always hit when we are up there together.

"And can I get a t-shirt? he asked.

Crikey, I think to myself, this is going to get expensive pretty fast.

"Yes, of course, it's your first music concert." I reply. He had done brilliantly at his mock exams. He had earned it. And I really treasured time with him, especially after losing Daniel. In fact, every year he lived past 12 was a win. I could feel my mindset shift slightly at this thought.

We arrived at the stadium after a long walk through London, with bellies full of Mexican street food and a bag full of Muse souvenirs. I was probably at least £100 down by now. But Levi was happy and I was starting to think sober music concerts were okay after all.

As we walked to our designated seats we passed the bar.

"Can I have a coke please?" Levi asked.

"Sure thing!" I reply, and we head over to the bar. As one of the first people in through the doors it was pretty empty.

With ease, I order two cokes. And then I see the menu.

Now, while I had kept up my music passion with small bands and little bars and pubs, I had not been to an event like this for many years.

Behind the server, on the menu, were the prices of alcohol drinks and beers.

My eyes watered a little. A couple of years previously there would have been no way in hell I didn't order at least a double rum and coke. And then go back for many, many more. My £100 spent on a couple of t-shirts and some good food looked tiny compared to how much I might have spent if I was drinking that day.

Years later, I still wear that £50 t-shirt with pride and I love the memories it invokes. I get to keep the shirt. But I would have missed most of the concert for double the amount of money if I had spent it on rum and cokes.

And that's another thing, too. I remember the amazing light shows, and the feeling when Muse entered the stage. I remember the incredible moment when Levi's eyes lit up with wonder at the light show before him and the bursts of fire and the vibration of the guitars on your face and skin, the atmosphere in the crowd… Ask me about any of the many big concerts I went to previously though, and I can hardly remember a thing. What a waste of money, eh?

I once paid hundreds of pounds to see Madonna at Wembley with a friend, that was MY first big music concert. I really want to tell you it was awesome, and that Madonna was awesome. Of course she was!

I watched the video of it a while ago. Sat on my sofa and watched the entire set. It really was amazing. But can I remember any of it from the actual event I paid hundreds of pounds to attend? Can I, hell! I think I remember a few tracks from the band warming up the set before oblivion. I remember talking about it with my friend for years afterwards, but making it all up. Or nodding vigorously at her statements, blindly, because I could not remember a single bit of it. There were more than a few events like that for me after Daniel died too. Many of which I cannot even remember where I went, or who I was with. Again, what was the point, eh?

More recently I went to a very intimate music gig to see Sophie Ellis-Bexter play. By now I had done countless music gigs without alcohol, but this one stuck in my head most firmly because it was not long after the Covid lockdown. As I sang along and clapped to her jaunty pop tunes, I found myself looking around and marvelling at how well she could get everyone up and clapping and dancing. And how happy we as human beings are when we are dancing, and singing, and together. It was really quite moving. Then she taught us all how to dance to her latest track, and we were all howling with laughter.

Afterwards we swayed to a a tribute band playing Dire Straights' music. Oh my, how we sang! It felt amazing to be alive, and to be free from lockdown. To be able to holiday again, and stand together, and have FUN. It was one of the best music events I have ever attended in my life. I was the only person in my group that did not drink, but it did not matter one jot. My friends all now accept I do not drink, and love me anyway. All the bars near to me have huge stocks of yummy alcohol-free alternatives - too many to choose from.

Later we saw comedians, such as Jason Manford, and we howled with laughter again until our sides ached and our cheeks were sore with grinning so much, tears rolling down our faces. That weekend was absolute perfection in the company we kept, in the entertainment we had, and in the drinks that were offered. I left that festival happy in my heart and soul, and glad to be alive. And I remember every clear-headed moment of it today with so much gratitude.

Take that, big alcohol marketers.

Holidays

Okay, so we have done pubs and clubs, weddings and big events, and music concerts. Here's a biggie… How do you holiday without booze? I am going to add something here, controversially, and lengthen it to "especially if you have booked all-inclusive."

I used to love a boozy holiday. As both my husband and I were self employed, I used to tell myself we had to go away a lot to physically remove ourselves from the workplace, which, back then, was our home. So, that was my excuse to go away four times a year to somewhere sunny and hot. We especially loved an all-inclusive holidays.

My last holiday with alcohol involved was fairly typical… a cheap self-catering apartment in Tenerife in the Canary Islands, which are just off the coast of West Africa. Pretty much guaranteed sun, volcanic black sand, mountains, cheap food, and even cheaper booze. Oh, and lots of nightclubs and bars.

We went as a big group of friends, and the kids were safely ensconced with grandparents for 7 delicious days of doing nothing but drinking, dancing and sunbathing. Oh, and a topless Jeep with a lot of singing "Barbie Girl" as we drove up the mountains to see volcanoes. Brilliant fun!

The week after I came back I was asked how my holiday went.

"Yeh - amazing fun!", I responded. My brow furrowed as I tried to remember any of it. Which bit was fun?

On holidays with the kids we would go exploring, play games on the beach, or dig big holes in the sand and then a channel to the sea so the water slowly filled the hole up as the tide came in (Daniel's favourite thing to do on a beach).

On this holiday we would wake up around 5pm each day, having missed most of the day, shower and eat, and then hit the bars and clubs. We drank and - yes - danced until 4am and then talked for a few hours about nothing memorable with a couple of beers until we fell back into bed, completely inebriated, and then we slept the day away again.

Now, Tenerife is not somewhere you go to to see historical ruins, but it is a beautiful island with so much to offer the holiday-maker. And other than the car trip on the first day, we missed the entire week of daytime activities. We never once hit the beach, and the pool got nothing but a cursory glance as we traipsed past it at 4am, feeling worse for wear. By the time I got home, I needed another holiday to get over the holiday! I also looked like crap. And we were all white as sheets, because, it was a sun-free trip until 5pm.

And you know what? I would love to say we had an awesome time every night, but given the group leaned heavily towards men, mostly they all got really drunk and started fights with other Brits, or just slumped at the bars watching people dance and occasionally waving a hand at an apartment companion as they passed. Sure, the first hour or so of each night was great, but as soon as the alcohol levels had crept up, I think we were all mostly just blackout drunk.

So, we all got home, and not one of us could remember the holiday. It was mid-August, that we stayed there, so it was not cheap. None of us felt refreshed, we were all hang-dog and ruined by the week. None of us enjoyed the next couple of weeks of work. One of us even lost their job! What a success that holiday was. Not.

You could argue alcohol stole the holiday from us. It stole a whole week away from us.

"Oh, but holidays with no alcohol will be NO fun!" I hear you cry from the other side of these pages.

Okay, then let me tell you about another holiday. Actually, my very most recent trip, to Tampa in Florida.

Now this trip was very different, even though it was with a group of very good friends again. Different friends. These were all fabulous human beings I had met after I had stopped drinking alcohol. They were fellow alcohol freedom coaches with This Naked Mind Academy. Naturally, not one of us drank alcohol, and this was the first time I had ever met them in person. Until then we mostly hung around with each other on Zoom.

We were a big group of around one hundred people from all over the globe, the United Kingdom, the USA, Canada, Greece, Germany, Australia… a properly International bunch of good people. We were gathering for a huge five day conference to learn a magical new technique that would help our clients drop the urge to drink even faster than before, so excitement levels were high. It was Spring Break, though, one of the most expensive times to stay in Florida, so we were mainly sharing an Air BNB in groups of three or four. At first it seemed like a strange decision, but the fact I was now, effectively, part of a sorority, in a house with three other fabulous women, it just made the trip interstellar good!

We studied hard during most of the days, and networked with our This Naked Mind colleagues, sharing tips and insights that would later elevate our ability to help people stuck in the addiction trap. We listened to teachings from experts in the coaching industry, including author, Annie Grace, who started it all. We ate wonderful food at lunchtime together. I do believe I managed to sample every culinary delight America had to offer. I had at least three pounds to lose when I got home. (Note to my American friends… You know cornbread is just cake on your dinner plate, right?)

"Ah!" you might cry - "This is not a holiday!"

Maybe, maybe not, but it felt like a holiday. Eight incredible days spent in a fabulous place with fabulous people, where even the days we worked and studied were beyond awesome, I would call that the best type of holiday!

In the evenings and on days we were not at the conference we ate in amazing restaurants, and my friends took me to supermarkets to go "grocery shopping", which excited me probably more than it should have! We walked by the sea, and as it was St Patricks Day that week, the sea was dyed bright green. The sun shone down on us, a cool April breeze kept us from being too hot, and the Florida air felt good.

Then we would all head to a cosy bar, and cram around tables, at least ten of us, but often up to 30 of us, and we would talk and talk and swig alcohol free beers together and laugh hysterically at each other's jokes and stories. The waiters would come around with huge trays of AF beers and spritzers for everyone, and we all sampled each other's drinks. We discovered loads of new recipes we liked, and we would then order them the following night. There was never a shortage of choice to be had.

Jumping into the SUV later, we travelled back to our beautiful little Air BNB, tired but happy and satisfied, and climbed into pyjamas before settling on the sofas in the living room to natter until late into the evening about the events and learnings of the day.

And occasionally, if Annie was feeling beastly that day, our homework.

I'm kidding, of course - homework was great. We would practice the new techniques on each other, keeping our coaching skills up, whilst getting free coaching ourselves. It keeps our minds free and our hearts happy.

On the last day before I had to fly home a group of my fellow students from another house took me out for proper American pancakes for breakfast. My gosh, they know how to do pancakes in America. Utter heaven, I could have eaten two more stacks easily! And then out for some souvenir shopping, and to a cookie shop where the cookies were stacked high with colourful decorations and swirly cream. And we sat in the sunshine and nattered until we had to head to the airport and go back to our homes.

Have you noticed anything?

Yup - despite the whole event being about alcohol addiction, drinking alcohol had not even crossed my mind, not even once. And yet, the laughter lines etched into my face will never go away from that trip. It was seriously the most fun I had ever had in a single week.

Okay, mood change, because you are here for advice on alcohol and grief….so here goes.

My least favourite holiday, but the one I hold dearest, was a week on a canal boat on the Oxford Thames river. It was paid for by an incredible bunch of people at Safeways, a supermarket in the UK, and it was the last holiday I got to take with my beautiful son before he passed away.

Daniel was incredibly excited about this holiday. He had been stuck in hospitals for months on end, and this was time for all of us to relax and just spend some quality time together. By now his hair had grown back from the chemotherapy, and even though the cancer had increased in its aggressiveness, he looked better than he had in over a year. It's so strange how that happens.

As we clambered onto the huge ten berth boat, Daniel chased his brother Levi around the boat and they squabbled over bedrooms.

Daniel was only kidding around with his little brother, he couldn't care less, but it was wonderful to hear their laughter. I climbed onto the boat with a heavy, exhausted heart. It had been such a tough year, and knowing the treatment had failed was weighing heavily on my mind. However, the sun was shining, the river and the surroundings were stunning, and I decided to make the best of it. I desperately wanted to get a bottle of wine, but I had to be on call in case anything went wrong with Daniel's central lines, and for his medication, and to keep an eye on Levi, who swore he could breathe under water. He kept trying to prove it. Hell, I wanted to drown myself in wine. When I think back on it, I feel crappy about it, but it's natural when alcohol has its hold on you, and I now know it was not my fault.

By day we fished, or drove the boat slowly along the canal, with my husband and his friend and Daniel opening and closing the locks, and attaching bait to fishing hooks. We were heading up to Oxford, my old home, so I could show Daniel and Levi all my old haunts. Daniel was allowed to drive the boat frequently, and there was many a time we ended up crashing into the river bank or into trees, and the men would hop out onto the bank to try and pivot the boat back into the canal so we could continue our journey. We stopped at pretty little pubs, and eventually reached East Street, where we moored for a few days to explore Oxford.

Every morning we were greeted by a gaggle of friendly ducks, to whom we would throw crumbs of bread and cake. My husband bought whole cakes for the ducks, and trained a few to waddle into the boat for treats, to the children's utter delight. Daniel decided he wanted to keep ducks as pets, but sadly it was never to be. The kids played "worms" in their sleeping bags, wrapping themselves up tightly and crashing into each other, falling about laughing hysterically.

It was bittersweet, and at the time I thought my heart would not allow me to enjoy the moment. But looking back, I realise it was not the grief, nor the pain that held me back from being present in the moment. It was alcohol.

Yes, you heard me. It was not my dying 12 year old son. It was the lack of wine.

My thoughts were consumed about when I would get wine. I counted the days until I could get home and buy wine, and drink it alone to drown out my misery. At home, medical care was easily accessible, and I had friends and family to support me. Here, I was on duty, and I had to white-knuckle my way through the week, to survive it even, until I could go home back to the loving embrace of wine and that blackout drunk feeling that erased all pain and removed the heaviness from my heart until I woke up the following day. I thought of it as a reprieve. Seriously, I did.

It did not matter about the dreadful hangovers, the hang-dry mouth, the purple teeth, the bleary eyes, and mystery pains in my chest that hung about particularly when I drank to excess. I had convinced myself that the oblivion from the pain of life at that moment was key to my survival, and, sadly, shamefully, that is where I stayed when I got home, all the way to the night my son passed away.

I missed most evenings of my last few months with him. I was not present. I was wasted, every night. And during the day, and during that holiday, I obsessed and complained internally about when I could have wine again. I was not present. I missed my last few months with my beautiful first born son.

Because of wine.

When we returned from the holiday, the kids were so much happier. And yes, I suppose I was too. But did I enjoy the holiday?

No, because I had spent most of it craving alcohol.

I think it is fair to say, that even though I did not touch a drop of alcohol it totally ruined that holiday.

Now I know it was not my fault, none of this was. Alcohol is addictive, pure and simple, and my brain was reacting in the way an addict reacts when parted from the substance. I knew no better, and I had no tools or tactics with which to fight the urges to drink. So I allowed it to consume me, to the extent that it ruined my last few months with my son. And it would not be the last time I did that. No, it would take a few more lessons before I properly learned how to escape alcohol addiction for good.

I have told you all of this, even though it shames me to the core, to show you that alcohol can ruin everything, whether you drink it, or if you simply crave it. If I can convince just one person not to travel down the same alcohol path I took when you are grieving, then I will be happy.

One last piece of advice for you. I seriously would not bother with all-inclusive holidays anymore. They are often priced almost purely on alcohol consumption so you will rarely get the value. But you will get a better holiday at a place with better quality food and accommodation, and you will often pay less for it because you are booking room only, self catering, or room and full board. Your choice, but I have found holidays a much better quality experience since avoiding all-inclusive resorts where I can.

Okay, hopefully you now have lots of tools to use when you take a break from drinking. Up next, are some tactics you can use when life gets life-y, which it often does, or when the grief, stress or anxiety threaten to push you back into drinking the bad stuff. Use it as your handbook into getting back to where you want to be. See you in the next chapter.

Chapter Eight

Tactics to help if it gets difficult

"Life is 10% what happens to you and 90% how you react to it."

— Charles R. Swindoll

Okay, so, you have decided to take a break from alcohol, and you have chosen some fun things to do while you are on your break. Next up, as promised, are a few tactics to help you if things get a little tougher.

Life is a rollercoaster, as someone once said, and we cannot have wonderful days every day. Especially when we are going through a tough time, because every little thing will remind you of your woes, even when it is not related. We are a raw and open wound, susceptible to re-injury. So we must prepare ourselves for when things get tougher.

Numbing the pain is very easy. Riding the pain is somewhat less so, I agree.

But this is what we were built for, my friend. To go through the good times and the bad times. It is what makes us who we are. And alcohol, being its insidious, addictive self, works badly for us here. Your brain recognises that numbing pain is very simple. It's in a bottle, after all. Just pour, drink, and done. It does not consider the aftermath of the drink. It only sends a message on what it thinks will help you in that very moment of time. Only you can tell it otherwise, and counteract those messages, by hijacking your thoughts and emotions.

So, here are some tactics to rid yourself of cravings, and get yourself back to feeling like you can take on the world again. Or, at the very least, quell the thoughts of your own brain and its terrible ideas. There are hundreds more, but these are a few that really helped me in my journey. I hope they help you too.

"Surf The Urge"

This one is a favourite of Annie Grace's - author of This Naked Mind. It also worked really well for me.

It is based on scientific studies by Sarah Bowen, that have shown that trying to ignore your thoughts and cravings does not help you, and it can even have the reverse effect.

Every time you have a craving, grab your journal, and do the following:

1. Write down what you were thinking immediately before the craving. What happened to you? Did you hear something? Or see something that upset you, or reminded you of something you would rather not think about? Write it all down in detail.

2. Ask yourself, would I feel better not thinking this thought? Or if the thought did not exist in my head? Do not try to stop thinking it, just ask yourself the question and write down your thoughts. Go really deep here. This activity is about becoming aware of your subconscious thoughts, Byron Katie-style!

3. Ask yourself, would you feel better if you did not have to think about drinking alcohol right now? How would you feel if you never had to think about this ever again? What would your life be like without this thought? Again, go deep, root out those subconscious feelings. Your responses may surprise you!

4. As the craving progresses and starts to wane, write down what you are feeling in your body, and where. Is it in your heart or your chest? Or within your throat? Or your stomach? Is it painful? Are you anxious? Are you sweating? Write it all down.

By being mindful and really focusing on the urge to drink, you are shutting down the part of your brain responsible for the craving. It also means the next craving will not attack you so vehemently. For me, after only the third time doing this, I found myself writing hardly anything before it went away, meaninglessly and without harming me. It was like a magic trick. Thank you, Annie!

Why does this work so well?

Scientist Sarah Bowen identified that cravings of an addictive substance build and rise, and then collapse back, like a wave. She is all over YouTube with several of her studies, often using smokers, and the studies are fascinating. I recommend you search her up and watch some of her videos. Using this every time you get an urge will build defences within your brain and its reaction to cravings that will stand the test of time. Or, at least until you no longer need them. Remember, what you don't desire, you will never crave. I am hoping that, by now, the shine has very much worn off alcohol for you. Or at least begun to wear off.

And the best thing about this tactic? It works on anything you crave! I found it super useful for the sugar urges that followed giving up booze. (There is a lot of sugar in those drinks!). And also for foods I no longer wanted to eat. It's a fabulous tactic, and I will be forever in Annie's debt for teaching it to me.

The 50 Percent Rule

This one is particularly good for those of us who drink due to stress or anxiety. It's also a bit of a life saver when you have just experienced the loss of someone you love.

Okay, so imagine a vertical line in your moods, thoughts and feelings, right in the middle of all of them.

Below this line, you start to feel unhappy, angry, stressed, anxious or upset. You might want a drink to take away the pain. Or to eat something unhealthy, or self-comfort in some other way.

Above the line you are happy, motivated, feeling positive and free from anxiety. You may work well at this level, or laugh more. You see everything in a better light. It's nice here.

On the line, you are neither happy nor sad. You are just okay. You function perfectly well, and carry on with your daily life without any real issues.

The trick with this tactic, is that the minute you drop below the 50 percent line, you stop everything, and I mean everything, even if you are at work.

Your one single function, now, is to get yourself back to 50 percent, or above.

I recommend you build your own list of favourites here, but some suggestions that worked for me are:

- Going for a walk outside, on grass, in bare feet.
- A quick walk around the block if you are in an industrial space with no grass. Even being outside in the fresh air helps, I found.
- Take the dog out for a quick run.
- Go to a safe space, and do ten silly star jumps. This one is best done in private, but if you are feeling brave, then go for it in front of people!
- Sticking your headphones on and blasting a playlist of really high energy, happy music you love.
- (Yes, really) Doing a quick burst of housework to loud music, singing loudly. This even helped *me,* a housework hater!
- Hit the gym for ten to twenty minutes, and exercise off the blues.
- Meditate for 20 minutes - super powerful, this one!
- Do a little yoga
- Find a quiet space and read your book for 30 minutes.
- Invest in a mindfulness app, such as Calm. Find a quiet space and focus on only you for twenty minutes.

The list goes on, I highly recommend you create a list of maybe twenty different things that will get you back over that fifty percent line.

The trick is to use it on all the little things in life. Things that irk you. You cannot, for example, walk the dog and get over your partners death. But you can go for a walk to get over the refrigerator breaking down. Or being yelled at over a mistake made at work. Doing this regularly will even improve your ability to get yourself back over the line. It gets easier with every use.

And if you feel awkward doing this at work, don't. Because once you are back over that line your productivity will soar, and you will be much better to work with as a colleague. You are doing everyone a favour, including your employer, by looking after your emotional state of wellness.

Be Kind in your Mind

We can all be pretty horrible to ourselves, in our heads. Sometimes that voice that admonishes us for our actions is very cruel and harsh. Most of us would never speak to a friend or a loved one in the same way we speak to ourselves. Often we will blame ourselves for things that are obviously not our fault, or beat ourselves up for doing something "wrong", or forgetting things. For a drinker, this just makes us want to reach for an alcoholic drink.

For example, when we wake up with a hangover, we think awful things such as:

- "You're an idiot. Why do you do this to yourself all the time?"
- "Ugh, you're weak and disgusting. You cannot even control the amount you drink."

- "You cannot be trusted. And you are getting fat. And now you look like crap. Loser."

Have you ever had thoughts like this?

Lasting change comes only from self-compassion. So fix that voice in your head, and if you catch yourself using the mean voice, grab a notebook or your journal, and do the following:

1. Write down what the mean voice was saying, in detail.

2. Write down what happened immediately prior to this happening? Can you see what triggered it?

3. Now write down: Is it true? Answer this question. Would it be true in a court of law? Or is there any doubt here.

4. Write down: Is there anything you could have done differently. Is it reasonable to expect this?

5. If your best friend or a loved one said they had done a similar thing, write down what you might say to them.

6. Now, turn it around. For example, if your thought was: "You're an idiot. You failed at your diet and ate that cake when you shouldn't have!" - Turn it around to something that says the opposite, but something you are able to believe is true. For example: "I ate the cake, sure, but it's one cake, it will not ruin everything. I am not an idiot, I simply had a piece of cake. Oh, and don't "should" on yourself!" (That last bit was from my good friend, and fellow coach, Judi! I love it and now I use it all the time.)

Make sure it is believable. For example, writing "I can eat all the cake I want" might not be believable, so your brain will reject this. You must be able to believe your turnaround.

If you get your turnaround statement right you will feel the benefits and the release almost immediately. You might start smiling, and feel lighter all of a sudden. If you do not feel weight lifting of you within thirty minutes or so, find another turnaround.

Do this every time you catch yourself being overly critical with yourself, and you will feel more freedom every time. This is a tactic that can cause huge shifts in your mindset and your emotions, which in turn will help you heal faster. Used daily, it will change your whole life!

Scheduling Time to Worry

Worrying is something a caring human does. There is nothing wrong with it.

But when you are in the throws of grief it can feel pretty overwhelming, especially if your loved one was very poorly before they passed, or if you were heavily involved in looking after your loved one during the process. In these cases, worry can cause dramatic changes in your mood, thoughts and feelings, and can even cause bouts of huge anxiety or stress.

In the years that followed the loss of Daniel it would cause me actual pain to worry about anything. Everything would explode into a huge surge of anxiety and abject terror, and my body would react violently. Once, my friend and I took the kids to a play park, and Levi got onto a ride that looked terrifying. I absolutely screamed at him to get off. All I could think of was that he was going to get hurt and die like Daniel had. It was completely irrational, but it was merely a reaction to the trauma I had experienced. My kind friend talked me back down gently, realising what was happening.

Remember, worry and anxiety is an imagined future fear, it is not real, if you can. Sometimes this is easier said than done when you have experienced a big loss in your life.

If you are being affected by this, then I recommend the following.

- Choose a good time of the day to schedule in a time for worrying. A couple of hours before bed is often a good one, because then you can do the work on the worries before sleep, and you do not have the distractions that occur earlier in the day. Fifteen minutes should suffice.
- Invest in a small notebook, or use a note app on your phone. Carry this around with you.
- When you notice yourself worrying about anything, note it down in your book or on the app, and tell yourself you will worry about it during your scheduled worry time.
- At the scheduled worry time, get your notebook out, and work on the worry. Is it true? How does it make you feel? Is there anything you can do to avoid the issue? Should you accept it as being true? How would you feel if you do not have to worry about this? See if you can form a turnaround on it, in the same way as you did in the Kindness exercise above.
- If you like, once the work is done, you can tear up the piece of paper, or delete the worry. I actually skipped this step, and kept them. It was remarkable, looking back on them, how little I

was worrying about. Remarkable, and of course completely understandable.

Reframe your mind to JOMO.

The experiment you are taking, being free from alcohol for a while, is something you should be incredibly excited about. Think to yourself:

"I *get* to not drink alcohol today!"

Many people approach a break from alcohol as if it is a hardship. But as we have seen, you save money, and your health improves. Both mentally, and physically. What is there not to love?

So instead of FOMO - think JOMO! The Joy of Missing Out!

You miss out on hangovers, making a twerp of yourself, and getting into silly fights with your partner. You miss out on losing £50 while you are out on a night out, or a night in the A&E department when you trip drunkenly and chip your elbow. And you miss out on all the mental anguish, anxiety and depression.

And yet you still get to go out and have a good time, and carry on with your life as normal. Just minus the booze.

I'd call that a win… JOMO!

Journal everything.

Whilst you might think of it as a bind to have to keep getting your journal out and writing in it, journalling is so powerful when you are doing something life changing, like this.

Firstly, it is a great way to tap into your subconscious, and remap those pathways in your brain. Writing it down has the effect of cementing it into your brain. If you simply think it, it does not stick. Writing it down makes it stick, and it is incredibly liberating.

Secondly, when you are at the end of your journey, long after you have hit level four - Alive - you can read back on all the things you went through. And you can give yourself a big hug for what you went through.

Why is this important? For two reasons:

1. You will forget this. All of it. Reading back will remind you of what a warrior you are.
2. When you are free, you might want to pay it forward and help others who are stuck in the same situation. Right now, you might not be able to see this. But I can assure you that once you are free from both grief and alcohol, the joy you will regularly feel is *unbound*. Often the first thing a lot of us want to do, is pay it forward, and tell the world what we have discovered.

See how you get on with those tactics to begin with. Like I said, there are so many more in an Alcohol Freedom Coach's toolkit, but these ones seemed to do particularly well with clients who have experienced some form of grief in their lives.

If you want more, it's worth checking out my resources on my website at www.zerofierce.com . They helped me immensely during my pre-coaching days, especially when I started out on my breaks from alcohol. Let me know how you get on.

Next, we deal with the big stuff - what to do if your partner still drinks, and 'triggers' that threaten to drive you back to alcohol It's almost like I have done this before, eh? ☺

See you in a bit!

Chapter Nine

What To Do If Your Partner Still Drinks

"If you don't like something, change it. If you can't change it, change your attitude."

—Maya Angelou

Okay, so maybe you have decided to take a break from alcohol. Great stuff! But what if your partner drinks? This is a frequent question we get from clients, and it is a situation I experienced myself, so here goes.

Imagine a circle.

1. In the centre, there is you. Yourself. Wonderful you.

2. Surrounding that circle are people you can influence. They might be your kids, your partner, or maybe friends and other members of your family.

3. Then, surrounding those people are things you have absolutely no influence on. This could be the weather, or people you do not know, or even war, famine and death. You can be aware of these things, but you have no influence on these events or people whatsoever. Maybe you are not even aware of them. They are 100% outside of your control.

Okay, time for a quick-fire quiz question….

Out of the above options, which ones do you have CONTROL over.

Yep, that's right. Number 1. You, and ONLY you. And that is all you will *ever* have control over.

So, your partner still drinks after you have decided to take a break. How unsupportive of them, surely!? How dare they?

Or… *So what?*

If they drink alcohol, you do not need to drink with them. I would suggest you could challenge the fact that you are even thinking in this manner. Is this even your *own* thoughts? Or is this your addiction talking? Is this your brain telling you to drink again, because it desperately wants the dopamine hit from alcohol? Really examine this thought.

Now take out a journal, or a piece of paper, and write down exactly how you feel. Where do you feel it. Is it in your chest? Your stomach? Your throat? How does this feeling make you act?

Does it make you stroppy with your partner? Be brutally honest with yourself here. Do you glare at them for being so unsupportive of your feelings? Are you short with them, or are you ignoring them? How does that make you feel? Do you feel good about being like this with your partner? I suspect maybe not. Write that down too.

Now think of other areas in your life. Are they supportive there? If the answer is a resounding yes, then it is *not* true that they are unkind, or unsupportive of your feelings, is it?

Try reframing it now. If you were talking to your best friend, what would you say to them if they had the same problem? Would you recommend they leave their partner for being a twerp? Hmmm. Perhaps you would not. How would being alone help them?

Finally, how could you reframe the thought: "My partner should give up drinking with me."

First of all, should is not a nice word. Secondly, why do they need to stop drinking if it is you who wishes to take a break? You cannot see inside their mind, you have no idea whether they have given alcohol a job to do. We only know what is happening inside our own thoughts and feelings. You are the one trying to change your journey for the better. Allow them to do as they please, because that is all you can do.

How would you feel right now if you no longer had the thought: "They should give up drinking with me. They are being unsupportive."

You would probably be relaxing and enjoying a movie with them, right? Instead of feeling all that awful resentment inside you, on top of the grief you are already feeling.

Reframe it again. How does this sound:

"I *get to* take a break from alcohol and see where it leads. My partner gets to do what they need to do, and it does not affect what I am doing. Maybe, if they see me happier and dealing with things better, they'll join me. And if they don't, then so be it. I *get to* be the one who wakes up every morning clear headed and feeling and looking great!"

If this does not work, try a lesser version of the statement, or something that works for you, until you find a good shift. Think of a ladder. At the top of the ladder is the ultimate turnaround statement.

Go down a rung to a lesser statement, something better negotiated that you can believe. Test it. If you feel lighter, happier in yourself, then it's job done. Well done. If you do not, then keep going down the ladder until you find your turnaround. This step is very important.

When I first gave up alcohol, my partner, still struggling with the loss of our son, was still angry, still very stuck. His drinking increased until he started drinking in the afternoons at one point, too. I heard him pouring a drink at 10:30am once. I rushed into the kitchen to check, and it was true. He was drinking in the morning. I felt like I was losing him too, and I was scared stiff.

It almost drove us apart, because I would be resentful and snap at him, or refuse to speak to him because he smelled of booze. I wanted him to look after me for a change! I was losing my best friend, in some ways, and I retaliated badly at first. How dare he not look after himself and cause me another loss!

That resentment continued, on and off, for years. Then, as I started training as an alcohol freedom coach, I learned about the science side of addiction and alcohol, and quickly I started to realise where my husband was. All of a sudden, the resentment just sort of fell away, like I was casting off heavy chains, and my heart and my moods started to lift irrevocably. It was one of the very first benefits I got from my training.

Suddenly, I had my best friend back. We were chatting and laughing again, and he even started to drink a little less, because he was less stressed as well, and liked seeing me happier. So much of what was wrong in my home life was removed, and what replaced it was happier (adult) kids, happier husband, and happier me. He still drinks, and that is his journey. I still hope he will one day follow me into not drinking, but that is his choice. If he decides not to, that is okay too. I love him for who he is. We have both come through a lot since Daniel died.

But the important thing to notice here, is that *he did not change*. It was great to have my best friend back again. And the only reason I had lost him, was my own thoughts and beliefs. It was my *thinking* that changed. I got my best friend back, purely because *I changed my thoughts*. Powerful stuff, eh?

That's right, my friend, it was *all* in my head.

So, we loop back to what I said at the beginning. We get to control precisely ONE person, and that is ourselves. And yes, that includes our thoughts and emotions. Look deep into yourself - are there any issues that might be caused by your thinking, too? Could your thoughts or emotions be driving you into wanting a drink?

Which brings me nicely on to triggers…

Dealing with other 'Triggers'

Okay, so we have covered our nearest and dearest. What about our besties at the bar?

As I have covered already, friends may have mixed feelings about you not drinking on nights out. Some will be really happy for you, and super supportive. Others may be a little less so, and we now know this is largely due to fear of either losing you as a drinking buddy, or it brings up fears within themselves. So let's cover this next.

If you are on a night out, and your friends are badgering you to party with them, it is important to recognise that *this is not a trigger*. Why? Because, you control *you*, they control themselves. They do not control you. Remember we can only control ourselves, and nobody else.

"But it takes willpower to say no to them!" You might argue.

So, let's take this as an example then. What is stopping you from politely, but firmly, saying "No thank you."

Maybe they come back with: "Awwww no fun!"

Your response could be: "So is it me you want to be out with tonight? Or the booze?" Jokingly, of course. Or not. Your choice.

If you prefer to keep a list of reasons at the beginning, practice these before you head out for the night. Visualise yourself making all the right choices. Things I have used in the past are:

- Taking antibiotics for an ear/chest/tonsillitis infection;
- I'm driving early tomorrow;
- Doing a charity no drinking month (if you get donations, you can really give them to charity. Win-win!);
- Health or weight-loss kick;
- You are volunteering to be the designated driver;
- Early start.

There are so many more. Practice saying them in the mirror before a big night out, it really helps, and stick to the ones you like best for the first month or so. People will soon give up asking or cajoling you to drink. They might even offer to give you a little petrol money for driving, or to pay for your non-alcoholic drinks. Free night out, anyone?

Quick note here - I recommend not using things like 'Lack of money' because often your friends will just buy you a drink. And if this happens? Quietly leave it on a table somewhere, or at the bar, and ask the bar staff for something non-alcoholic. It has happened to me a few times. It is not an issue.

Now, you do not owe anyone an explanation about why you are not drinking, just to be clear here. A simple "it didn't suit me anymore" will suffice. And if people press you, asking if you had a problem, you can shrug it away: "No", you laugh, "It simply doesn't suit me anymore."

"Oh, are you an alcoholic?" This is becoming rarer, but it can happen.

"No, it simply didn't suit me anymore."

Honestly, I think over the years, this one has worked best at shutting people down quickly. They'll get over it.

Can you see how these sorts of circumstances are not triggers? Nobody is forcing you to drink anything. You can do this.

Cravings

Cravings can be a bit tough if they hit in an area you can easily access drink without thinking too much. My advice to you, is "ride the wave of the crave". Or use the tactic 'Surf the Urge', if you are at home and have a journal handy. If you are at a bar or on a night out this might not be so easy to do.

So, play with it. Really think about how it feels. Is it uncomfortable? Does it hurt you? Is there any genuine pain? Where are you feeling it? What does it feel like?

We do so much to avoid the discomfort of a craving, but why? I quite enjoyed surfing the urge to drink after a while. It was surprising how brief it lasted, especially as the days went on, and how un-scary they were! I used to be terrified of them and give in to them almost immediately. But you control your thoughts and emotions. You can ride this out.

If you can, writing things down, even if its on your phone, really helps too. And it's awesome when you read back, a few weeks, months or even years later. It was like looking into a time capsule, and when I read mine it made me feel so impressed with the me of years ago for doing this. I was pretty badass back then!

Remember, your brain is simply signalling to you it is dopamine time. You can tell it to pipe down. You don't want to drink today. You are trying this out. Butt-out with your wrong-tool advice! And then find something else to occupy your brain with. The feeling will pass almost as quickly as it came.

Missing the Ritual

This was a huge one for me at the beginning.

When I first gave up, I found myself really craving alcohol. Or so I thought. Then someone suggested I might be missing the ritual of getting home from work, and having a drink to relax in front of the TV with.

So, I tested this theory out, and purchased a few alcohol free treats. I chose a couple of pale ales (very hoppy tasting, yum!), and some pre-mixed alcohol free G&Ts. I made sure I had plenty of ice in the freezer.

On the first night I created a perfect alcohol-free G&T, with oodles of ice, and some cucumber curls. I served it in a huge gin glass, sat down in front of the TV, and watched a movie with my partner.

Well, what a revelation! It was exactly the same! No cravings felt at all, I got the same relaxed feeling, minus the hangover the following morning. The beers did the same, so I bought a few more varieties, and when I had found my favourites, I dedicated all the space in the wine fridge to my alcohol free goodies. For months I would enjoy taking time to choose whatever I fancied from my excellent selection of drinks, and relax in front of the TV or a game. I got exactly the same effect as I had always done with alcohol. This discovery was so profound. After all the worry about giving up alcohol, or, as I was doing at the time, taking a break, and in the end it was a doddle!

I definitely recommend this to everyone who drinks to relieve stress or work anxiety.

A few people have asked me if low alcohol (0.5%) is cheating. My response to this is: You do you! I personally still drank these too. The weird thing is you will find yourself drinking one or two a night, because they do not have the dehydrating effect alcoholic drinks have on you. But even if you WANTED to try and get high on them, you would need to drink something like 32 of them to even get a mild buzz. You would more likely be sat on the loo all night instead of getting drunk, as there are not many bladders that could take that quantity of liquid for very long!

If you are stuck for ideas of recipes for alcohol free cocktails, or some nice booze-free drinks to try, then head over to my website at zerofierce.com/recipes. You will find a multitude of delicious things to try. They are so sublimely awesome, and tested personally by me, you will not miss the alcohol at all.

Boredom

This one was perhaps the hardest challenge for me when I was giving up alcohol. Boredom.

If you are used to filling every evening with alcohol, getting more and more squiffy, until you head off to bed, boredom could hit you. You suddenly get a huge amount of time to yourself when you first give up. It's amazing, but you might not immediately appreciate it.

Good news: You can use this time to do anything you want! Take a course, read, paint, draw, play games, exercise, take up Yoga, volunteer for a charity, the list is endless. But if you do none of these things, boredom may strike. And this might trigger you to want to drink alcohol.

Consider this: First of all, what is so interesting about alcohol? And why will it relieve boredom?

Are you actually bored, or are you longing for the numbness and loss of feeling from the pain of grief or disappointment, or stress, or anxiety? Yep - you've got it… Journal it. Write it all down.

Remember, journalling it will help your brain reason with itself, and it will help cement new patterns and new habits. Write down ALL your feelings and thoughts. Where are you feeling it? What does it make you want to do? How do you act? Get it all down on paper.

After you have done this, DO something. Anything. Walk in the garden in bare feet, tidy up, do a few dishes by hand, play music and dance around the room, do a few yoga poses, play ball with the dog. The choice is yours, just do this until the feeling goes away.

Being bored is a luxury many can never afford to have. Enjoy it. Sit in the moment and listen to your surroundings. Breathe. Feel the moment keenly, and be thankful for three things in that moment. Be present. Feel lucky to have your health right now.

Alcohol will not help you. It will hurt you.

You can do this.

How alcohol hinders - my story

When Mum told me she had been diagnosed with breast cancer I felt numb. My whole body went into shock, and then it shut down. To me, cancer was a death sentence, and it had not been all that long since I had lost Daniel. I shook as she told me about the prognosis, but I put on a brave voice and tried to speak in a positive manner. The worst thing was she lived 400 miles away, in a little town called Cockermouth, so supporting her would be so hard. And, of course, she had lost Dad all those years ago. I was worried she would be all alone for the entirety of her battle against her illness. Tears poured silently down my cheeks as I spoke on the phone to her. My Mum was so brave, I did not want to make this any harder for her.

Initially I disappeared further into addiction. Alcohol still, but now I added food into the works as well. I did not care anymore. My lovely mum was poorly, and it was the worst type of breast cancer, the one which was super aggressive. She would start her treatment immediately.

I am ashamed to say I did not race to Cockermouth to be with her. Part of the reason was work commitments, but I could have gone occasionally. I guess the other part was fear. I had seen what cancer could do to people. I was petrified of being in its shadow again. Mum insisted she was okay, and she did have lots of friends around her, and colleagues, and they were a wonderful bunch of people from what I had heard.

I was drinking even more by now, and hearing mum was poorly had made me even more miserable. I spiralled into bad food by day, and too much booze at night. By now I was barely going out, other than to work, where I was functioning absolutely fine. I was tearing up my work projects, smashing targets, getting promoted regularly. Anyone looking at me would think everything was fine. I probably buried myself in work, too, often working weekends and evenings as well to ensure all my targets were safely met each month. It was not a great way to live, to be honest. Looking back I am fairly certain that I had added work to my growing list of addictions.

Once Mum had finished her treatment, she would regularly drive down to see us. And once a year we would go on holiday together, but now we were going to places like Cornwall instead of abroad. Mum, as a breast cancer survivor, could not get travel insurance for overseas holidays without paying ridiculous excess fees.

If she visited us on the South Coast I would, on occasion, call a taxi to drop her back off to her hotel so it did not impede my drinking time. How awful is that? If I had delayed my first glass of wine by a few hours I could have dropped her off myself. My addicted brain would feel slight panic that my routine was interrupted, too. This massively spoiled my excitement of seeing her.

The holidays and visits were awesome, but, again I am ashamed to say, I would spend most of the day thinking about when I could drink wine, counting the hours to 7pm. I loved the time we spent with mum, we were lucky to keep her for another nine years after treatment, before she lost her battle aged 69. Looking back I feel I wasted every evening I had with her getting drunk, and with her looking on in concern. Mum never said a word, but you could tell she was worried. I hate that I did that to her towards the end.

Did alcohol help me in this time? During her illness, and after her death?

Like hell it did.

It stole precious time away with her. It meant I was not present for her at a time she needed me. I was too busy self-medicating and feeling sorry for myself, and being a ball of anxiety, to notice she was getting sick again. And I was too busy getting hammered every night, and the wine was too important, for me to jump in the car and drive up to her. So I missed her last few weeks due to cowardice and choosing wine and inebriation over her last few days. I spent the days feeling hungover, depressed, overweight and miserable, and everything around me crumbled. All because of wine.

On the day of the funeral I was supposed to read a eulogy to the mourners, many of which were her friends from the charity she worked for, and her old work colleagues. But I was hungover that morning, and a mixture of hangover and absolute fear meant I decided not to do it less than hour before the service. I told the vicar I would prefer it if she read it in place of me. And at the wake, my brothers and I drank too much, and we did not speak to many people after the first hour or so, preferring to spend time together, all of us now adult orphans, consoling each other. We were a close family, and losing Mum hit us all hard. We all three of us put on brave faces, and we drank a lot as the afternoon wore on.

Going back to work after Mum died was not great for me. I worked in a high stress area of the business, and by now cracks were beginning to show. And it became even worse when, helpfully, along comes perimenopause. This, together with alcohol, was to later help me on my way to complete burnout.

Alcohol was beginning to harm my moods and my anxiety levels as well, and I would often have to stand up and leave the office when jibes or bitchy remarks hit home. When the Managing Director told me something wasn't "good enough", I ran out of the room in tears, and the Head of Finance mopped me up with a million tissues as I cried for an hour straight. It was definitely not one of the finer moments of my career!

When I went home each night, out came the bottle of wine, and I had started to increase my drinking to two bottles on some nights. Occasionally I would want to blank everything out so badly, I would drink myself into complete oblivion, and my husband would carry me upstairs to bed. I did not care. I had lost my lovely Mum, and my son, and my Dad, I wanted the world to open up and swallow me whole. Life felt completely and utterly unfair.

Honestly, I cannot think of a single way in which alcohol did me any good. Even though it managed to numb me, it usually hit me so hard I would pass out, drunk, and often woke up on the armchair, with a stiff neck or shoulder, and unable work out where I was. It was lucky I rarely went out by this point, or I could have put myself in real danger. My blood pressure was now very high, I was having palpitations. My annual private medical tests were beginning to flag the warning signs of a heavy drinker.

I booked an appointment with the doctor and they warned me about my drinking levels, even though I had lied about how much I was actually drinking, and also my weight. They put me anti-anxiety medication and blood pressure medication, but refused me hormone replacement therapy because my Mum had died of hormonal breast cancer. I did not heed the warnings though, as I felt unable to stop drinking now.

I decided I might flip my drink again, as I was liking the wine a bit too much, and switched to gin, which a lot of my work colleagues were enjoying. I chose a premium brand, deliberately making it an expensive one, hoping that would slow me down, but of course I soon got a taste for gin too. Up went my drinking again, and the health costs related to it, and up went the anxiety and depression as my dopamine levels see-sawed.

Sometimes I just want to go back to the woman I was back then and give her a massive hug and tell her it would eventually be okay.

I had periods of alcohol freedom, where I would stop for a decent amount of time. But each time I would forget how bad I felt when I was drinking, and something inside me decided I could start drinking again and not get stuck. During one of those periods, an extended one, I even managed to get motivated enough to clear up the house, sell it, and buy one in a better area. I wanted to get out of the city, where all the hospitals were that reminded me of Daniel, and all the landmarks we had visited with friends and family we had now lost. I wanted a fresh start, so we upped sticks and moved to a beautiful island nearby. But I brought alcohol with me.

It was wonderful in the new home. No more reminders to drag us down all the time, and a beautiful beach nearby. We went on long walks and I joined a weight loss group and made new friends. But every night I was drinking too many gin and tonics, or glasses of wine, and I was not losing much weight. I was happy though, life was getting better. But something was beginning to gnaw at me.

I felt like something was holding me back, and I was missing out on something really important in my life. It took me a few tries at things before I realised alcohol was the problem, and that was when I started my journey to give it up altogether.

Does any of this make you feel like making a big change in your life? Or perhaps you are thinking about taking a break from alcohol to see what all the fuss is about? Next step in this journey is all the wonderful alternatives to drinking alcohol. Get excited, and jump in to the next chapter with me!

CHAPTER TEN

What to do instead of grabbing a drink

"Fulfillment isn't found over the rainbow—it's found in the here and now. Today I define success by the fluidity with which I transcend emotional landmines and choose joy and gratitude instead."

— RuPaul

Okay, so let's face facts here. We are all different. The things that cheer me up when I am having a rubbish day are probably not the same as things you would enjoy. And this is good! But I would be skipping a whole, important chapter in this book if I skipped this one.

So, bear with me, and suspend your imagination for a bit. The goal here is to open up your mind to the possibilities. You mind may be a little closed right now, especially if your loss is very recent, or exceptionally painful.

I am here to show you that it is not your fault for looking to alcohol to remove yourself from your pain, but that you are simply using the wrong tool. Your brain thinks it's the answer. It is trying to look after you. But it is suggesting the wrong tool. So allow me to show you how to reach a place where you can begin to choose a better tool with which to lift yourself out of the grieving process, and in a less damaging way.

Doing the math

Okay, let's start with one that might cause you resistance. It was the least fun for me, but by far the most beneficial for my mental wellbeing. Exercise.

I have always been a bit of a digital Queen, loving all things tech, gaming and computer orientated. So when spin biking company, Peloton, came out with a bike which was linked up to a screen and live classes, it was my exercise dream. It was gamification of exercise. There were challenges, and award badges, and beginner levels and lots of options for your choice of music or trainer. It was perfect for me. Except, it was over £2000 at the time. And I did not have £2000 to spare.

So, I stuck it on a credit card.

"What?" You might be asking, "This is not good advice!" And you would be right. Getting into debt is never the answer, but this is why I did it:

First, I worked out how much I was spending on alcohol every week, like so:

Seven Days of my favourite premium gin and a nice but not cheap Mediterranean tonic:

£39 + £7 + £39 + £7 + £39 + £7 (half of £39 + £7) = £161 a week.

(Cucumber not included, because I ate that instead.)

Even looking at that today, I shudder.

So, monthly, that was (£161 x 4.3) = £692.30

Minus the monthly fee for the bike @ £39 = £653.30

Bike Costs = £2200

Bike can be paid off in 3.3 months, plus a few weeks for interest.

So, a humungous, considered purchase. One that would later go on to give me amazingly toned legs. It would help me lose weight, keep fit and lower my blood pressure and resting heart rate, for *years*. And it would replace just over *three months of drinking*. Are you kidding me?

All I had to do was not drink my favourite gin and tonic for three months. And I could have this wonderful, luxury purchase.

But I needed a little extra motivation. Back then, I loved my gin! So I signed up for a 90 day alcohol challenge as well. I was going all in!

I rode that bike every single day for 90 days, and I did not drink. I smashed the challenge. It was easy! All it took was for something to be worth more to me than that half bottle of gin and tonic each evening.

But then weird things started to happen elsewhere in my life…

Firstly, I was getting compliments on my appearance a lot, especially a month into my challenge. When I looked in the mirror, even I could see the improvement. But I figured it was the extra exercise I was getting, rather than pinning the reason on lack of alcohol.

Secondly, within weeks of being without the booze, I gained the confidence to apply for a new job. I loathed interviews and putting myself out there, properly loathed them! But when a job caught my eye, I applied without hesitation, and wrote the most amazing cover letter too.

As I sat in the car outside of the building where I would take the interview, I thought briefly about turning back and going home. Just then, a sweet little robin red-breast flew down onto my windscreen wipers and stared at me with cute beady eyes. For at least a minute, we just stared at each other in silence. "Brave robin!" I thought to myself. They were usually very shy. And then it tweeted and flew off.

I shrugged it off and got out of the car for the first interview.

Within two weeks, I had not only been invited to a second interview, but I was offered the job. They almost bit my arm off! I am rubbish at interviews usually - just a ball of nervous energy and lack of confidence and forgetfulness. My perimenopausal symptoms had not helped my career at all thus far. But, this time, I had aced both of my interviews with ease. I know it sounds silly, but I still think that my Mum might have sent me a message through that little robin. It calmed me, made me less anxious.

Within a week of the job offer, my existing employer offered me a 25% pay rise, added me into the bonus scheme, and gave me free private healthcare, rather than allow me to leave. They never did this usually, and to my knowledge have not done so since. My confidence soared, and I had no idea what to do with it. Next step was a to and fro battle to win me over, which I still cannot believe to this day. I ended up staying with my current employer, with promises of extra staff to help me out with my role, management opportunities, and more.

It was an amazing 90 days with no alcohol. Life changing! But I still did not put any of my newfound luck down to giving up alcohol.

So, bike paid off, challenge completed, a pay rise… What to do next?

I went back to drinking. That's what. And very quickly I was back to drinking the same, if not more, than I was before. And life got life-y again, and slow. I still went on my bike, but I was not getting the performances or benefits I had previously. The weight loss stopped, because wine contains so many empty calories. There were no management opportunities at work. And on I plodded. I felt okay, because I had done my challenge. There was a small, nagging voice in my head that told me I was heading for trouble. The issue was I still thought alcohol had something to offer me. I had not yet completed my emotional journey, and had only dealt with the behaviour, which, as you might know, never works.

It was only later I would identify that the 90 days had been incredible due to a *lack of alcohol*, but still, it gave me 90 days off, and that was still a brilliant thing. I think if I had worked out the reason for my life upgrade was alcohol, I would have definitely not re-started my drinking.

So, am I saying you should all rush out and buy a £2000 exercise bike? Hell, no!

All I am saying, is do the math. If there is a course you would love to do, or a dance class, and you aren't sure if you can afford it, work out how much less you would need to drink to be able to buy yourself this adventure. Because, trust me, *anything* you do will be more fun that sitting on your sofa knocking glasses of wine back whilst sat in front of the TV.

Courses in just about anything can be bought online, just for fun, and you might find something you fall in love with, and maybe you even switch careers. Or learn something you have always been curious about. One of my clients started a course on reading tarot cards, and another decided to learn to write poetry. Both have continued to enjoy these as hobbies ever since. And the poetry is really good. She has even been published recently.

Open your mind to everything. Suggest to a friend you might like to try something new, and ask if they have any suggestions. You may have never thought of paint-balling, go-karting, Kung Fu or ballroom dancing, but why not give it a try? Most classes offer a free session.

The second time I gave up, I knew the answer would be to flip something in my life. I was still enjoying the Peloton bike, so that would not count this time. I asked my husband what he fancied, and he replied: "I have always wanted to learn how to keep bees."

Oof. I was not keen on insects. But, brave head and big-girl pants firmly on, and with no better offers, I signed us both up with the local Beekeeping Association and their next beginner course in Beekeeping.

For ten weeks we attended evening classes, and it was the first thing we had done as a couple since losing Daniel. Steve was great, making himself available for every class, and I think he even started to enjoy the social side of things a tiny bit. He was not keen on meeting new people normally, but our fellow beekeeping students were such interesting people. All of them shared a lot of our eco warrior beliefs, and we all liked bees of course. Steve came out of his shell a little, and looked forward to the day he could get his bees. I have a new-found respect for the honey bee, they are amazing creatures. Vital to our planet too.

I am proud to say I am now the proud owner of a felt patch badge, a certificate, and over 90,000 bees! I still have no idea how that happened, but it's a great community, and we get to do our bit for the planet. The world needs more beekeepers, and it wasn't overly expensive to set up our first hive. Certainly it was cheaper than a month's worth of gin and tonics! Again, I did the math, I took up a new hobby. I now look pretty dapper in a beekeeping suit, and I know how to identify an Asian Hornet. It also did a lot for my fear of insects. Win, win, I say. I highly recommend this one, even if you only do the training. Give up gin, save the planet!

I was feeling a lot better without alcohol again. This time around I recognised the pattern. I started to look healthier, like I had been given a "glow-up". My teeth were whiter, hair thicker, eyes brighter. I received another small promotion. Mysterious things started opening up for me, potentially because I was allowing the space for them to come into my life instead of drowning out the signs with expensive white spirits. I was completely alcohol free and over the moon about it. I didn't even crave the stuff! And the relationship with my husband got better and better as we took on a new hobby together. Bees were his thing, though. I needed to find my own thing.

Massively Multiplayer Online Games

I was always a gamer, from a very young age. Ever since my Dad had come home with a computer for my brother and I: a glorious Dragon 32. We loved that computer so much.

I had disappeared into *World of Warcraft* after Daniel died, and I was lucky enough to have a legion of friends who followed me in there. Partly to hang out with me, and partly to make sure I was doing okay. Many of them ended up staying, they enjoyed it so much. One of these people was Steve's best friend, Terry.

Terry was a lovely man, strong and kind and super brave. He and Steve had grown up together since young children. They lived next door to each other from an early age, until they both left home to move into their own homes with new families. When I came along, he was warm and welcoming, and a fierce protector. He became one of my best friends in the world too. Everybody loved him. He was also there for Daniel when he became poorly, taking him to see football matches, or to drive racing cars. Terry was part of the family.

We would all play *World of Warcraft* for hours every night. *Warcraft* is a massively multiplayer online game, where you pay a small monthly fee to play with millions of other players all over the world. The community is amazing, and, if you find the right group of like-minded individuals, it can be a Utopia. You are accepted no matter what race, sex, size or financial bracket you belong in. You are just appreciated for being you. And we were all lucky enough to have found a bunch of crazy, funny individuals, all around the same age. We all had families and jobs, and all of us enjoyed an evening or two a week killing big bosses together and making each other laugh. Terry, whose character in *Warcraft* was known as Scart, was popular and well-loved. He would help any player in need of help, and was a staunch supporter of anyone in our 'Guild', or group of players.

Sadly, Terry worked on demolition sites for a time early in his young life, and as such had breathed in crumbling asbestos dust. He was diagnosed with aggressive cancer when he was 50. His illness progressed fast, and perhaps mercifully, it killed him within weeks. We were all devastated. Many of those who attended his funeral had only known him through *World of Warcraft*. So many of them turned up in person to say goodbye. We even had an online service in the game for him.

I spent many good years in that game with my friends after Daniel died. That world was a much better one that the real world that awaited me when I logged out. But I was also drinking a lot as I played. So, returning to it after the bee-keeping course felt a little strange at first, without the alcohol. And it felt like something was badly missing without Scart. But I received a big welcome back, and quickly I re-learned how to play the game I had loved so much.

I discovered that gaming was actually a really enjoyable way to spend an evening when you are struggling with grief, *even* without alcohol! In fact, I was a lot better at playing the game too. I soon found myself invited to groups frequently, quickly becoming well-known for my ability as a good, reliable healer. And I loved to collect all the colourful flying dragon mounts. I would soar above the world, flying all over the lands on my dragons to find new quests and adventures. Even sitting in one of the pretty tree-lined lakes, to fish and natter to guild mates, was an enjoyable way to de-stress and spend the evening.

Again, something wonderful occurred in my real life. A senior manager at the company I worked walked over to me one day, and asked if I played *World of Warcraft*. He had heard a rumour from my manager that I did.

Alarmed, I blurted: "Yes, but it never affects my work!" (*World of Warcraft* players of old were known to be often late to work, usually due to late night raids and drinking with guild mates all night.)

"Me too." He replied, to my astonishment. And invited me to play along with his friends that evening.

He and his friends were brilliant at the game, and I soon became fast friends with him at work as well. They all joined the same guild I was in eventually, and we smashed through the content with tears of laughter rolling down out faces. It was an excellent time of my life, and it probably didn't do my career any harm, either. I had started to enjoy my work life as well, and he championed me for challenging projects. He knew I was reliable and did not give up easily through the way I played the game and ran the guild. I am still good friends with him today, and while he was at the same company he made it super good fun and bearable. He even became my boss for a while - one of my best bosses *ever*.

These online worlds are vast and varied and they are a wonderful way to pass the time, and cost very little each month, once you have a decent computer to play them. The computer you need can be a fairly high cost purchase. It costs around £10 a month for the subscription, and is perfect for adult players and casual gamers to relax in. If this does not float your boat, then consoles are cheaper and there are lots of single player adventure games to sink your gaming skills in to. Or VR Headsets are available for a very reasonable cost, and many games can be played while seated so you avoid the dizziness and crashing into walls.

I wanted to include gaming as a lovely way to disappear into something for the first few months of not drinking, or to use as an alternative space while you are grieving. It's also a great way to make new friends. And, to remember lost ones, too. Sending love to Terry, or Scart the Mage, however you want to remember him. RIP, our wonderful, kind friend. xx

Charity challenges

It is not uncommon to pair your break from the booze with a challenge. There are so many to choose from. You can of course choose the month-long drinking challenges such as Dry January, Dry July, or Sober October. But why wait? I recommend a non-drinking challenge that might improve your mental health or improve other people's lives in some way.

Some of my clients and friends found the app, Couch to 5K, a big motivator, and took up running. Not my thing, but they all experienced their own "glow-up" of sorts as the weight just fell off them without the booze and with all that extra exercise. All of them found that they were mentally far stronger, and better able to deal with the loss of their loved one.

Those with younger children discovered parkrun, where you could meet up and run, or walk if you had a pram or a dog, around a set route. They are held all over the world, and they are free. Another client of mine started these two years ago, never went back to drinking alcohol, and looks ten years younger. She now volunteers for parkrun events all over the country and helps other new starters. She even runs the odd marathon for charity. If you had met her years ago, you would never recognise her as the fun, zesty human being she is now, all because of signing up for a weekly free event at her local park, and giving up a particularly expensive habit in drinking cocktails in the evenings. Her next target is sugar, but between you and me, I think she probably halved that when she gave up the cocktails.

I am not keen on exercise, especially running, but I did sign up for a month-long charity Step challenge. I loved Step class in the eighties and nineties, so thought it might be fun to try again, and I wasn't wrong! It was great for all levels, and usually ended at the juice bar where we would all sit and natter afterwards, so I also made some new friends. We raised a lot of money, but the memory that sticks in my mind the most, was when my best friend saw someone she knew in the gym.

"Oh, my! Look at you, I hardly recognised you!" She cried. The lady in question stopped, turned, and grinned at my friend happily.

"Tracey! Ah, lovely to see you, and thank you. I have lost three stone!" She replied.

"How did you lose all the weight?" asked Tracey. "Did you do Weight Watchers or something? Which diet did you do?"

"Oh, no, nothing like that." She replied. "I just gave up wine."

As this beautiful, slim, blonde bombshell walked away from us, we looked at each other in astonishment. Amazing, the results some people get when they ditch the wine.

Immerse yourself in a new venture

This is the reason I am here with you now. Free from alcohol, and knowing I was never going back, I decided to take a new direction in my life, and train to be an alcohol freedom coach. I wanted to give something back. I wanted to help people like my brother get out of the alcohol trap. I was unhappy in the corporate world, and feeling like my age was going against me in my job as a digital marketer, and my colleagues were getting younger and younger by the minute. I also knew I wanted to be self-employed and be my own boss again.

Initially I looked at franchises, and lots of training courses for all sorts of subjects, and nothing quite sat right with me. At one point I quite fancied driving around in a white van, delivering pet food, and at another I decided I could teach kids how to cook. For over two years I looked into several options, all of which would have allowed me to work for myself again. None of them quite ticked all the boxes though.

Then *This Naked Mind* wrote to me, as someone who had successfully completely one of their courses, and invited me to train as a coach. I have no idea what happened, it was as if one of my loved ones was leading me, but I signed up on the spot. Nothing had ever felt so right to me!

No matter what it is you love, be it a degree with the Open University, a new college course, or an online creative writing module… Find something you can completely immerse yourself in, something you will enjoy doing. Whether you take a new direction with your career, or simply add loads of new knowledge to your fast-healing grey matter, choose something you'll enjoy learning about. You never know where it will lead. And without blotting out your thoughts and feelings with alcohol, your new-found creativity could very well set your whole life alight!

Volunteering for a few hours a week

"Hard times don't create heroes. It is during the hard times when the 'hero' within us is revealed."

—Bob Riley

This quote by Bob Riley resonates so strongly with me, because it reads so true to me. I cannot begin to tell you how many remarkable people I have met since training to become an alcohol freedom coach. People who never stop broadcasting the beauty of a life alcohol and drug free, and inspire others to follow.

Before my training, I found myself with a few extra hours to spare in the week. I had just attended a Digital Marketing conference in Brighton, and there was a speaker there who suggested we all donate our digital skills to a charity or cause. I thought this was a brilliant idea!

I found a lovely UK cause, called Loaves of Love. They were in need of a Social Media Manager, which was one of the jobs I had done for the company I worked at. Serendipity worked its magic once again, and it turned out the people running the charity worked at the same company as me! It was a perfect fit. I worked on baking and food channels, and this was a baking and food-based charity!

It was a great way to give something back while doing something I enjoyed doing. And it fortuitously brought me back to working on Social Media, which would prove useful later on in that year, unbeknownst to me.

It does not matter what your skills are, there are so many roles to play for local charities, I heartily recommend this as an excellent way to move through your grief instead of using alcohol. You will meet others, some of whom will make you feel very fortunate indeed. And you will be doing someone the utmost kindness with your time, all in the name of your lost loved one.

What a wonderful way in which to honour them, and to make them proud.

Losing yourself in something sedate

I still believe many of us turn to alcohol when we are grieving or stressed, because we need something sedate in which to sink in to. This was certainly true for me, and for many of my clients. But as we have already seen, alcohol is not the right tool to use.

So let's next look at more sedate options. These can help enormously by putting us into a more mindful state, a state of reflection, which is very healthy, mentally, and a good place in which to move through your grieving process.

One of my coach colleagues started making music. He used to love clubbing, back in the day, and his music is upbeat and euphoric, just the sort of thing I love. One of his tracks is particularly good for housework, which I loathe doing, but I seem to be motivated enough to get started with his track on my stereo. I am definitely not marking *this* up to serendipity though, because I still hate housework. But his music is now available to download on Apple Music and Spotify, and he has hundreds of followers who enjoy it. I love listening to his latest tracks, and, secretly, love the fact I have a DJ friend.

Another coach I met paints, and his paintings are available at shows and exhibitions. He gave up alcohol and picked up a paintbrush, and now he makes a living off of the proceeds. Previously he was an architect, a job which he found stressful and made him unhappy. Remove the alcohol, and he is an artist. And his work is really very good!

Other options include writing. I had wanted to be a writer for years while I was still drinking, and would often do a course, or try to break into it. But alcohol shrinks motivation and douses our dreams with a poisonous arrow. It also shrinks the parts of your brain responsible for carrying messages, and kills brain cells, so there are fewer cells to do the job it used to. All you have to do, is drink more than the government "recommended amount" of 14 units a week. You do not need to be a so-called "alcoholic". You could argue alcohol kills human creativity.

Without alcohol, and with my new-found skills I had trained in, I started writing a book, and it actually came to be. In fact, you are reading the results right now! This very book has realised all my dreams of becoming a writer. Hopefully it also realises my dream of helping people, or even one person, who is facing the same uphill battle I once did. Let me know if it helps you, and it will be my circle completed.

Another thing you can do, is simply go to bed earlier, and read books. Lots and lots of books. And dream a lot.

Alcohol kills your ability to read well, and to sleep. Both of which were my two favourite things to do as a child, long before I started drinking alcohol. And they are one of the best things I have discovered about being alcohol free. I found I could return once again to my favourite things.

Nowadays I read copious amounts of books, and in doing so I constantly improve myself. I also sleep wonderfully, for around eight hours every night. Proper sleep, not like the REM-free passing out of old, followed by waking at 3am full of angst, scrabbling for my phone. Even a single glass of wine a week can badly disrupt our sleep.

My friend, the dreams are magical when you are alcohol free. I regularly spend time with the loved ones I have lost, and when I wake up in the morning, it feels so real. I feel as though I have said hello to them again, after missing them for so long. A few nights ago, I saw my lovely son, Daniel, who looked exactly the same as when he did just before he became poorly. He was laughing and happy, and delighted to see me and tell me about his time in a place I cannot remember. He didn't stop nattering to me! Just like he used to. I awoke with tears on my cheeks - good tears, and I felt genuinely as though I had spent a little time with him. I felt comforted. I have have no idea what that was, but it is not the first time it has happened, and I know in my heart it will not be the last.

So, I hope some of that gave you some inspiration as to what to do next. The choices you have before you are literally limitless! You are a powerful, creative human being, and the world cannot wait to see what you will do with your new alcohol-free super powers.

You might be asking, what about moderation? Or after I have healed, can I go back to drinking alcohol?

Read on for my thoughts on this very subject…

CHAPTER ELEVEN

Moderation, and moving on

"It is never too late to be what you might have been."

— George Eliot

What about moderation?

A lot of clients ask me about moderation. It is one of the most common questions we are asked, collectively, at the This Naked Mind Institute.

Mostly, this is due to fear of giving up. They worry their lives will be dull without their alcohol crutch to lean on, or that all the parties will just stop. They have no idea how life will look without alcohol, because, quite simply, they cannot remember a time when they did not drink it. Many spent most of their teenage years looking forward to being able to legally drink it in pubs, or even started drinking early in their teens, and then never really stopped. Going out to a pub? Order a beer, a glass of wine, or dash of spirit in a mixer. It was all automatic. Social acceptance almost demanded it.

Driving? Be sad, cue hang-dog face, order a coke. Complain a lot.

But some people genuinely want to get alcohol back under control. Back to when they could take it or leave it, and shrug it off, instead of feeling like they are white-knuckling it all the time.

My experience of moderation was: it was bloody hard work. Much, much harder than stopping. When I was moderating, it was okay, but I found myself thinking about alcohol constantly. I would think about it all day, looking forward to my two drinks, which I had by now pushed later into the evening so I didn't get tempted to drink more. And I did not really enjoy the two drinks I had, because I was drinking to numb myself, and two drinks numbs nobody. I was effectively still missing out on the experience I had grown used to over my decades of drinking.

I resented it too. I resented the fact I still wanted it. It created far too much conflict in my brain, and I did not like the fact it still had a hold on me.

So, encouraged by previous breaks, I decided I wasn't going to bother with it anymore, after reading a bunch of quit-lit books and doing a course of group coaching sessions. The freedom in my head was absolutely heavenly!

Seriously, not having to think about it ever again, not wanting it, and alcohol not even figuring in my life, was so invigorating, it was way better than anything those few drops of ethanol ever gave to me. I would walk past the wine aisle in supermarkets with pure joy in my heart, and a lot more money in my pocket. Fewer shopping bags to carry, too! Food tastes so much better too, without alcohol. So I decided to buy better quality ingredients for my recipes because I am saving so much on the cost of expensive gin. I now shop at the local farm shop in Hayling Island and buy more organic produce, and I still save lots of money. I treat myself to premium ingredients and healthy food choices.

At This Naked Mind we see clients who drink only at big events, such as a wedding, and then never again unless they are invited to other events, and they are happy with this. And a colleague of mine has a client who drinks exactly once a year, a couple of whiskeys with his father, on his birthday, because it's tradition. He doesn't touch it at all for the rest of the year, and that is his thing.

The key thread here, is getting to a place where you do not want to drink. To, as Annie Grace, author of This Naked Mind, says: "make it small and insignificant." What you don't want, you never crave, or even think about. Or care. When I knew I was drinking too much, but wasn't sure how to fix it, which is a painful, horrible place to be, those words were like honey to me. I really wanted that, and I found it. And, my friend, it is every bit as good as it sounds, and more! It was SO good, it was the main reason I trained to be an addiction freedom coach with the Institute, so I could give something back to people who felt as stuck as I once did.

The key is getting to a place where alcohol is meaningless and does not matter anymore, where the constant battle within you ends, and you do not care whether you drink or not that day. And you might drink one or two, and you might not. And if you don't drink that day, you might not drink again tomorrow. Until suddenly, you haven't drunk any alcohol, or wanted it, for three or four years! And your life has changed entirely, for the better, simply because you stopped drinking those few insidious drops of addictive ethanol. It has no power over you anymore. The feeling of freedom fizzles through you like a delicious, fizzy thing.

How likely is it that you will be able to moderate and be happy? Well, the This Naked Mind Institute did an efficacy study, which showed that out of people who participated in their coaching methodology, 36% went to successful moderation, cutting down their alcohol consumption considerably, and they were a lot happier since. 54% gave up alcohol entirely, and did not drink again. That, my friend, is a 90% efficacy, where rehab and other plans have success rates in single figures. The reason? If you don't want it any more, you simply do not think about it. So you are not white-knuckling it. You just don't care about alcohol anymore. The plan deals with your thoughts, feelings, and emotions, and not just your behaviour. That is the secret sauce to its success.

Mindful drinking, which is one of the tactics I use often during the first few coaching sessions with my clients, is where you proactively, and without judgement, ask yourself questions while you drink alcohol. For example, do I actually want this drink? Do I need it? How is it making me feel, and how long for? Has it improved my mood, or have I deferred any problems until the following day in doing this? If the drink made me feel better - when did it start lifting my mood? Was it when I started sipping it? Or was it sooner, as I was pouring it, or opening the bottle? It's important to study everything and journal everything, and the answers you find are often surprising. Those answers challenge what you believed to be true beforehand, and in challenging your beliefs, you can make new thoughts and beliefs which better serve you.

Me? I was happier being completely free. It was a bit like smoking… I hated smoking, I gave it up, I enjoyed not smelling of cigarettes and not having to pay silly amounts of money for it, and so I never went back. It is that simple.

My final time moderating did not exactly go to plan.

I had a Christmas party to go to at work, not long after I had decided I would moderate. It was wonderful - a masquerade, and I had some fabulous colleagues at the time so I was looking forward to it a great deal. The venue was swish, with walls full of huge paintings of people staring down at us, sweeping staircases, and enormous hallways with painted ceiling arches resplendent in gold. There was music, and dancing, and delicious food. A fabulous well done for a good year of solid hard work.

The wine poured freely for all, but someone on my table knew the manager of the venue, so they were particularly attentive to us. Every time each of us took a few sips of wine, the glass would be topped up again. Now, this is not an excuse, I knew I was drinking more than the two glasses I had promised to myself, but somehow my brain convinced me that it would all be okay, and I would stop when it was needed.

And do you think I stopped?

Hell no, I did not. We all progressively got louder and louder, and drunker and drunker, howling in laughter at each other's jokes, yelling across the tables, and taking selfies together. It was cacophony! Any idea of moderation slipped away as the evening progressed. It ended up with me being bundled in a colleague's car as they tried to decipher where I lived from my very drunk self. I woke up the following morning with a cracking hangover, and so many regrets. I decided that day to just keep drinking, because I was a complete failure. And sadly, I drank even more than before. This would happen each time I moderated, without fail.

The only drink you ever need to say no to is the first one.

It would be several months before I re-read the quit-lit and finally gave up for good. And from the day I made the decision to just quit altogether, the freedom I felt was enormous. All of that fighting inside of my head just disappeared, all of the blame, the shame, the constant telling offs I would give myself, all gone. I knew, without a shadow of a doubt, that I was done with alcohol, and I felt as though I could finally breathe a sigh of relief. I had no idea what that decision would mean for me, and how good life would soon become.

Why can't I drink normally?

I have often been asked by clients: "Why can't I just drink like a normal person?"

My response is always the same. You are normal. It is normal for every one of us to become addicted to alcohol, eventually. We all will if we keep drinking. Some of us hasten that process by giving alcohol a job to do, that is all. Now, many challenge me on this. "I have drunk two a night for the last ten years, no issues. I can control it. I am not addicted."

Okay then. So, why not stop?

It's a substance your body does everything it can to get rid of as soon as it enters your system. In fact, it stops most other processes, just so it can focus on getting rid of the poison you just ingested. This is part of the reason alcohol is carcinogenic. So why drink it in the first place, when it does so much harm?

"Ah, no, I like the taste of it." They'll reply. Or it helps them relax, or de-stresses them, or they've 'earned it', or [enter any reason here].

The facts are, it does none of these things, and you had to acquire the taste of it before you could readily drink it, because it's foul tasting poison. But they don't want to give it up… because they do not have a problem with an addictive substance. Just like smokers can stop any time they like, they just don't want to. Hmmmm…

So, if you find you cannot moderate, you are one hundred percent normal. You are human. It is not your fault, it is the fault of alcohol. This is why the messages on UK adverts for alcohol annoy me so much. "Drink Responsibly" they say. Really? And how are we supposed to do that? Drink an addictive substance "responsibly"? It's as if they are putting all the blame on the customer who bought the alcohol, and they are. Great customer service, Big Alcohol.

It is also much harder to give up alcohol than it is to give up smoking. Alcohol is the only drug where you have to have a good excuse when you decide not to drink it anymore. If you were giving up smoking, you would get a big well done! But friends will try and talk you out of giving up alcohol. Also, alcohol marketers are one of the biggest spenders in the industry, and they spend billions on glossy advertising that we are surrounded by everywhere we go. The next time you watch TV, count how many times alcohol features in soaps and dramas. Or games we play. It's a constant no matter where we look.

So, if you have a hard time moderating yourself, or find yourself going back to drinking time and time again, stop beating yourself up about it. It is not your fault. It is alcohol. Period. And what's the first thing you want to do when you feel crappy? Yep, you're right - drink! So enough of the voice in your head telling yourself you are not good enough. You would never speak to a friend like that, so stop talking to yourself in that manner too.

Should I try alcohol-free drinks? Or is that cheating?

The next time you are out with friends, I definitely recommend you give an alcohol-free alternative a try. Choose something close to something you drank before going alcohol free.

"What? Isn't that just as bad? Won't it encourage me to drink more, or trigger me?"

Nope, it is fine, and there are loads to choose from nowadays. In as little as two years we have seen some amazing alcohol-free beers, ales, gin, wine, and mocktails hit the market, and some of them are gorgeous! Make sure it's how you like it, too. So, if you love a bottle of beer, make sure they have chilled it. If you love a mojito normally, try the alcohol free alternative, but remember to ask them to make it with the ice, and the lime and the proper glass, in the same way they would treat an alcoholic drink. And then, open your mind, and really enjoy it.

I absolutely love an alcohol-free drink at a pub, and I'll try loads of new ones if they have them there. Plus, you will find you do not need so many, without the dehydrating effect of alcohol, so you will save heaps of money to boot.

Should I count my alcohol free days?

This is entirely up to you, my friend. I chose not to, but I know hundreds of people who love to dig out their counters and celebrate milestones.

For me, alcohol had genuinely become SO small and insignificant, that I simply forgot about it. I know it was a few years ago now, but I do not know what month it was. I did not even know that my last day of drinking alcohol was going to be my last day! No memory of that day either. And it's utterly fabulous!

I also have friends and colleagues who celebrate their anniversary of giving up drinking alcohol, or the centenary (100 days, 200 days, etc.) of their last drink, and good for them! It IS something to be celebrated. Most of us have spent so long languishing in the mess alcohol creates, we deserve a big pat on the back for knocking it on the head.

And then I have colleagues who have not given up drinking. They can drink as much as they like, when they want to. They simply do not want to drink anymore. They never say never, but right now, alcohol is nothing to them, and they wouldn't have it any other way. And this is super important… If the feeling of never drinking again scares you, at first that's fine, and normal! It is just your brain trying to protect you, and the status quo. It thinks you are benefitting from your nightly alcohol binge, so it might buck against thoughts of you quitting forever.

If this happens, I strongly recommend you simply tell yourself: "Don't worry, it's just for today. And if it goes okay, I might not drink tomorrow, either. This is an experiment, so let's be patient and give this a try. I want to see what happens without it for a bit."

Then, each day, decide not to drink that day, and embrace it! Embrace waking up every morning without a hangover. Embrace being able to drive to work without worrying in the back of your mind whether you are slightly over the limit in the morning. Embrace not worrying you smell of alcohol, or are acting strangely when you pick up your child from the Christmas Disco later that night. Embrace how clear your eyes look, how white your teeth are, your bouncier hair, trimmer waist, or in noticing the little aches and pains that used to plague you are no longer there. And definitely embrace all the extra cash in your bank account. I cannot believe how much healthier my finances are. I am even able to put money into savings now! Remember, the spending was never just alcohol, it was everything else you purchased with it, and the taxi rides, and buying rounds for others, and losing money when you are tipsy, and buying extras at supermarkets so you aren't just buying booze. The Jack Vettriano paintings. It all adds up to way more than you would like to think! I do still hanker after that Jack Vettriano painting though… It was called *Back Where You Belong*. Oh, the irony. Hehe.

So, my advice to you on counting days, is: You do You. :-)

Celebrating the little wins.

Ah, this is, for me, an important one. Whether you are counting days or not, always celebrate the little wins. You are doing an awesome, amazing thing. You are bucking the trend, swimming against the tide, going against the grain. You deserve kudos for this! You are badass AF!

So, maybe a week in, buy yourself a little treat. Or a big one! Calculate how much money you are likely to have saved on alcohol alone, and add a bit, and then spend it on you. Even if you never spend money on yourself, give yourself a well done gift. And then do it at regular intervals.

The reason for this is as follows: A big part of giving up alcohol is delayed gratification, and our brains are not the best with delayed wins. We are impatient for the good stuff, which is why you may have fallen off the wagon a few times before giving up, whether you are taking a month break, or longer. It's a long time for your brain to go without any sort of gratification for what you are doing.

For me, I bought the odd game on Steam, or a book I had wanted to read for ages. Another month, and I joined a gym, because I wanted to feel better all round, and I was feeling motivated by my progress. Another month, and I bought myself the spin bike, because I had fallen in love with spinning, which did not feel like exercise as I was enjoying it so much, but I hated sweating and going bright red in front of people. As I have already said, it wasn't cheap, but I traded it for another three months off booze, which easily covered the cost of it. And I succeeded, because I was rewarding myself for my hard work with good things.

I have now been drink-free for several years, but I still reward myself. For example, if I see an amazing pair of boots I fall for, I buy them. Those boots, at £70, cost about the same as a week's worth of gin, or a single night of drinking in the pub a few years ago. So I buy the boots, and I wear the boots with pride, because I am not using that £70 to drown my sorrows in booze.

And always remember, what you are doing gives you your money, and, most importantly of all, your health back, especially if you managed to stop drinking before it made you ill. After all, our health is the single most valuable thing we have.

Glimmers

Ah, now this was a part I was looking forward to writing as soon as I started this book. Glimmers! Oh how we love you!

What are they? Let me tell you, my friend, glimmers are THE most incredible thing a non drinker discovers, and it is usually a big surprise because most of us did not even know they existed previously!

Triggers are false friends. They only exist in your head. Your partner drinking does not "cause" you to drink. What they do, and what you do, are two completely separate things, you cannot control any of it in any shape or form. Pictures on the TV do not trigger you. They are just pictures. Triggers are just thoughts, and are your brain trying to get what it wants, which is an addictive substance. Never give in to them without understanding it is YOU that is doing the action, and it is not the fault of anything else, except perhaps alcohol.

Glimmers are the opposite of triggers. And this is what makes them so amazing.

Say you are going for a walk, and this happens frequently for me. You look around, and suddenly you are filled with the most wonderful shiver of happiness, pure joy, that you are alive, and free from booze. Free from all the cognitive dissonance. Free from worry and shame. You are FREE and you feel *fabulous!* This is a glimmer moment!

Or maybe you are at work, it's a mundane day. And at lunch you look around at your colleagues, and suddenly realise how lucky you are to have all of this. A job, good colleagues, money to spend, a good meal in the staff canteen… the list goes on. You just stop, for a moment, and experience time as it is *in that very moment*. And it feels wonderful to you. Glimmer!

Or when you are with your children, and they are playing a game they play frequently, and suddenly you are caught by overwhelming love for them, even more than you have ever felt before. It's so pure it fills your entire body, and you feel wholly grateful for everything in your life, just for that one moment of calm. Glimmer!

These things never, ever happened to me when I was still drinking. But now they happen all the time, and my life is so full of joy and happiness and gratitude. It's almost spiritual. And my fellow non-drinkers will agree, it makes you sad for those still trapped in the alcohol maze, even if it's a few drinks a week, because even a small amount of alcohol can steal your glimmers, and what you could become without alcohol. Which is why so many of us decide to try and give something back, and spread the word.

I cannot wait for you to experience glimmers too.

Sleep and your health

Glimmers aside, this is one of my top, top benefits I discovered when I gave up those few drops of ethanol every night.

Sleep! Delicious, wholesome, sleep, with dreams, and everything!

Do you remember sleep when you were a child? Probably not, but I do. I used to LOVE going to bed with my book, and I would read for bit, before falling asleep in soft terry sheets, and I loved to dream. It just felt so luxurious. I was very lucky with my childhood.

Well, let me be the first to tell you, it exists as an adult too! I tend to go to bed earlier these days, and relax into a good book before falling asleep almost instantly, and dream about so many things. I usually sleep all the way through to the following day, and I wake up feeling refreshed and revitalised and ready for the new day. Ugh, it's fabulous!

Sure there are still life's little issues when life gets life-y. But I would say that, after the first week or two, sleep became the most precious gift of all of the gifts I found after giving up booze.

And you know all the odd flutterings in your chest you felt occasionally when you drank, the missed heartbeats, the shooting pains you worried about? They all went away. So quickly, I did not realise they were gone until someone else complained about them! "I used to get those too!" I thought to myself. And then I realised they were all gone.

How about menopause, eh? Or perimenopause? My gosh, what a beast THAT can be.

Anyone who can relate, the hot flashes, the night sweats, vastly reduced after I stopped drinking. It was like a wonder drug! And to think I used to drink wine because I thought it helped get RID of the symptoms I was experiencing in perimenopause! It turned out, almost all of them were exacerbated by alcohol. I lost so many of them, it felt like I was 'me' again, after years of suffering the often debilitating symptoms of perimenopause.

Bloated face, dark circles around your eyes, spots, stained teeth, aches and pains in your wrists, shoulders and knees? Mystery backache nobody can give you the reason for? Stiff neck? Give up alcohol, and you might find you lose these too.

I always had really short eyelashes. I never linked it to alcohol at all, but when I gave up, they grew and grew and grew. Now I can actually sweep mascara onto my eyelashes and my eyes will really pop! And my fingernails are finally strong and healthy and require minimal work to keep them looking shiny, healthy and pretty, even without nail varnish.

They don't stick all this on a bottle of gin, do they? But if you were told you would lose access to all these basic things about being alive, you would never touch that bottle again. Funny how the alcohol adverts never show the morning after, either. It's all marketing lies.

Motivation, and life changing events

There have been so many amazing experiences for me, now, since I stopped drinking.

But I refer again to the conference for the *This Naked Mind* Institute, with over one hundred people, in a hotel in Tampa, Florida. It was packed full of the most amazing human beings I have ever met, many of whom are now firm friends, my TNMI colleagues. All of us had our stories to tell, we had all suffered in the struggle of wanting to be free from alcohol, and having achieved it, we all wanted to give something back, spread the word, and help other achieve the freedom we had found. The room was absolutely electric every single day of those five days, and it was one of the best experiences of my life.

I would never have experienced this if I was still drinking wine. Not even if I had managed to cut back to two glasses a week. I would still have been stuck, and still a slave to alcohol and its effects.

Paying it forward

I have no doubt that you will reach the place you want to be with alcohol. I also have no doubt that in a few years, ten at the most, a younger generation will look at the amount of alcohol we drink as a nation and across the world right now in disbelief, in the same way kids today cannot image the smoky pubs and clubs we used to hang out at in the eighties and nineties. Or how you could smoke at your desk while working in an office. But until that time comes, some of us will continue to spread the word about the amazing life you can live without alcohol.

I had no idea a few years ago that I would end up training to be an Alcohol & Addiction Freedom Coach. None, whatsoever. I saw the callout from Annie Grace's *This Naked Mind* Institute, whose book had been important to me in my own journey, and something inside me just clicked. The original plan was to help my younger brother out of the trap too. And then to help others as well. I had given up alcohol for a while now, and the improvements in my life, my health, and my finances, was so huge, I wanted to help other people struggling with alcohol because they too had given it a job.

The process was pretty selective, they were looking for only the right people, and on the day of my interview with *This Naked Mind* Institute, I received a phone call to say my little brother, and one of the people most central to me in my world, was in hospital. It was not good news.

I decided to go ahead with the interview, and signed up. I honestly believe my Mum and Dad guided me to that place, and guided me in making the investment in myself as well. It was a level of decision I have never taken before in my life, and one of the best decisions I have ever made.

I headed up to the hospital, which was around 100 miles away, that very week.

My brother was unrecognisable. I almost walked straight past him, but our youngest brother recognised him immediately and gave him a hug. If I hadn't have brought him with me, I would never have found Alex without a nurse pointing him out. His face, his whole body, was bloated, his eyes sunken. Handing over the magazines, nibbles, and

and fruit we had bought on the way to the hospital, Alex told us what had happened.

It started with a cough he could not get rid of. Then his arms, face, and legs swelled up, and he could not breathe. They rushed him into hospital, and after emergency tests, the doctors asked him if he had life insurance, and how his wife and young kids might be looked after without him. No messing around, he had oesophageal cancer, the cause of which is commonly related to drinking alcohol. Alex was not a huge drinker, but a nightly one, like I used to be. He was high-functioning, a great Dad, and husband. A funny, wonderful man who looked after his big sister and called her every week for a natter. He was my go-to guy for advice. He was so clever. He was my rock.

I sat down on the end of the bed and looked at him.

"We did this to ourselves, I guess, didn't we, Dee?" He said sadly. I nodded. I had not started my training yet, so the tendency was to blame ourselves. We all do. "You must fight this, of course." I demanded. Alex agreed, his wife had told him the same, so he would, he said.

And he did. He took the chemotherapy, the radiation therapy, and all the drugs they gave to him, but just as with Daniel, it made little difference. He had small cell cancer, and it meant it was almost imperceptible as it roamed around his body. And the COVID-19 pandemic had meant nobody had taken the cough very seriously, and the waiting lists meant it had already gone metastatic.

Alex fought really hard in his short, but intense fight with cancer. But after six months, he lost his battle, and passed away peacefully in his sleep in a hospice near his home. His passing broke all of our hearts, and left two beautiful, and very young children, fatherless.

My friends, I was there with him as much as I could be, given the distance between us. And I was there with him the day before he died too. He asked me a million things a big sister should never have to answer, we were very close. But I was present all the way through for him. Every night, every day, we would text, and joke around, and email, and call each other. And at no point in time did I even consider drinking, even though my world was, again, collapsing around me.

At his funeral I was present for everyone, standing at the front of the room, and then I was present for his friends and family. And I did not even think of drinking alcohol at the wake, even though it was held in a bar.

And for the months afterwards, as I grieved and often cried, I never thought of going back to drinking. And I was present for everyone. Not being brave, just being *present*. I held space for everyone who needed it, and they held space for me.

And occasionally, when the pain became overwhelming, I would cry, and I would allow it to happen for as long as it needed to happen, until the tears stopped of their own accord.

Sure, the pain hurt me, inside my heart, my chest, my throat, behind my eyes. It hurt like hell.

But I can tell you, right now, that the pain felt cleaner, almost, and the grief passed through me faster, like it is supposed to. It did the job it needed to do, and I mourned the loss of one of the people I loved more than anyone else in the world. I still cry sometimes, even now.

Without alcohol, and in giving grief the space it needed in my life, the process was - yes - _easier_.

It felt better, so much better than any of the times before. And I could be proud in knowing that I held space for my lovely, funny, baby brother, and that I was there for him whenever he needed me, and whenever it got hard for him, and for whenever he lost hope. I was there for him, cracking bad jokes, and writing rude things on his notes, or leaving bad drawings and scribbles on his medical board in hospitals. He sent funny pictures and jokes to me, every day, and I sent rubbish jokes and silly memes back to him.

My friend, when I lost Daniel, my Mum, my Dad, I did the best I could with the tools I had back then. I did not know it at the time, but the most damaging tool possible was alcohol. It dragged me into addiction, and I did not even know it was addictive. I thought it was a shortcut to getting rid of the pain, but all it did was add to my pain and lengthen the healing process. Human beings are built to feel, think, and experience everything life has to offer, be it good or be it bad. Alcohol took all of that away from me until I was able to walk away from alcohol. *It will do the same to you.*

In the end, in losing my beautiful brother, I learned the *only* way to grieve, is to experience it fully in all its forms. Vividly, rawly, to open yourself up and allow it to tear you apart. Because after it is done with you it heals you right back up again. The only way, dear friend, is through.

Never be afraid of grief, never hide from it. Someone important to me once said that to grieve was considered by many the ultimate form of love, because you are mourning the passing of someone who made a difference in your life. Celebrate that, cry and cry and cry those tears, and do not let an alcohol brand, who makes millions out of your suffering and mine, who leaves children fatherless, who destroys lives… *Never* let them take that away from you.

I qualified as a coach a few days before Alex passed away. And I called my new coaching business: ZeroFierce. Zero, because zero alcohol, and Fierce, because I was going to throw rocks at my enemy - Big Alcohol - for taking away so much of my life, and for taking away my baby brother.

I hope you see hope in my stories. Especially this last one.

And that's it! We are all done. I hope this book helps you, even if it's in some small way. Let me know - I love getting your messages.

If you have any questions, then feel free to drop me a line at amanda@zerofierce.com, but, if not, then you've made it! You should now be chock full of tips to get you through this, without leaning on alcohol. Forearmed is forewarned, as my lovely Mum used to say!

Consider yourself shielded against the monster that is alcohol addiction, but the rest is up to you. Getting addicted to alcohol is never your fault. But it IS your responsibility.

Read on for some extra help and resources, and then, my friend, it's time to release you into the wild. Remember to allow yourself cry. Those tears and emotions are there to be spent. Not to be drowned away in alcohol.

Love and safety to you in this tough time, and a big huge hug. It *will* get better, my friend. It will.

Amanda x

CHAPTER TWELVE

Putting It All Together And Further Help

"Character cannot be developed in ease and quiet. Only through experience of trial and suffering can the soul be strengthened, ambition inspired, and success achieved."

— Helen Keller

You still here?

This is excellent news. It means you are serious about achieving your new life without alcohol!

So, if you need further help, here are a few extra ideas.

Alcohol Freedom Coaching

Or, in other words, the best job in the world! I am a fully certified TNMI Alcohol & Addiction Freedom Coach, and it is my goal to help as many people as I can out of the alcohol trap. Due to my experiences, I have an extra speciality in grief coaching too. If you struggle to get yourself to a good place, then I, or one of my lovely colleagues, can help.

If you would like to work with me, you can book a free 45 minute session with me via my website at www.zerofierce.com/booking

In the session we will look at where you are in your journey, and how we can move you from Awake to Alive! The best, and most life-changing place to be, by far.

The *This Naked Mind* Methodology offers incredible efficacy rates:

- 90% of respondents have decreased alcohol consumption, or are no longer drinking at all after coming into contact with the program.
- 86.5% of respondents noticed their mental health improved significantly.
- Over 1.1 Million *This Naked Mind* books sold.
- Over 400,000 people completed the 30 Day Experiment.

[*Internal survey research based on 2936 respondents and evaluated by Dr. Marilin Colon, PhD.]

Hiring a 1:1 Coach is the Gold Standard investment in yourself. It goes far beyond a course or challenge. A coach is on your side, and will champion you to get the results you desire. All of them. It was life changing for me, and, if you are willing to be coached, it will be life changing for you too.

First of all - let's cover what a coach is not. A coach is not a medical practitioner, unless of course, we were a doctor beforehand. We are not psychiatrists, nor counsellors, nor therapists, all of which tend to deal with past trauma.

A coach is an individual who has mastered something you would like to have in your life, and shows you the way through to success. You do all the work, but the coach has an overriding view and the knowledge of how to navigate the path to success. For me, that is showing you the way to free yourself from alcohol, either by controlling it, or by giving it up altogether, and making it so small and irrelevant you literally do not think about it, care about it, or want it.

A coach will champion you in your journey, will see the path ahead clearer than you are able to, and will help you as you travel that road. They are your confidante, someone who listens to your stories, your feelings and your thoughts, and helps you navigate those. Even those thoughts and feelings you feel unable to tell anyone else. They help you find turnarounds that make you feel instantly better, stronger, and able to face life's daily problems with new-found confidence. This is what my coach did for me.

Have you ever been caught in a loop of wanting change, but never being able to achieve it? Or perhaps you have tried over and over again to change something, such as drinking alcohol, and you keep slipping back in to it a few days, weeks, or months later. And each time you slip back into drinking, you seem to drink even more? Do you occasionally use alcohol to drown out the noise of the day, get rid of stress, or hide from something worse, such as bullying at work, or the loss of a job. Do you feel anxious or depressed after drinking? Are you losing sleep?

Millions of adults feel exactly the same as this, even if they do not tell you as much.

If you find yourself stuck here, and you are looking for a way out, then this is where a coach can work their magic, and set you free.

Imagine yourself five years from now if you do not change something. Is this how you want to feel? Now imagine yourself ten years into the future if you do not change. Fifteen...

Now imagine yourself in ten years where alcohol is small and irrelevant. You can take it or leave it. You simply do not care about it. Your health is better, your life and relationships are better. Dream Big! Now imagine yourself like this in five years... One year... How about 12 weeks? Yes, it's absolutely possible for you to be free in 12 weeks, I promise! And even sooner if you wish. In fact, it's possible for you to be free as soon as you want it.

Success could be yours much quicker with a coach on your side to show you the shortcuts to the place you want to be. What is that worth to you?

FREE RESOURCES

I have lots of free resources available to you - simply head over to my website at:

https://www.zerofierce.com - Options offered are:

- Regular free ebooks, workbooks, or courses for subscribers.
- Lots of FAQs and interesting studies on alcohol.
- Recipes for alcohol free cocktails and reviews on the latest alcohol-free drink options that are out there. I update this regularly.
- Links to support and free courses.
- My blog, where I muse about the latest in our alcohol free world.
- And lots more!

Head over to the Free Resources section of my site for more information.

Subscribe to my emails

Subscribe to my email list for all the latest on a wonderful, alcohol free life, and lots of tips and tricks to get there easily. Plus, subscribers get exclusive access to competitions and giveaways, and regular freebies.

Follow me on Instagram and Facebook - @Zerofierce

I love a new follower - don't we all? Follow me on the socials and I will try and make you laugh on occasion. I am even on LinkedIn, if you are not keen on the main channels. If you are funny AF I'll follow you back.

Your next book recommendation

I would be seriously missing a trick if I did not recommend Annie Grace's fantastic book - *This Naked Mind* to you all! I read a lot of quit-lit when I was going through my journey giving up alcohol, but this book resonated with me the most, and for that I am forever grateful. Head to my website for other great reads!

Oh, and if you love a podcast, *This Naked Mind* has an awesome one. Buckle in, though, there are hundreds of episodes and counting… It's a fab source of info to sink yourself into when you decide to take a break from alcohol.

Give something back.

Finally, when you have reached that wonderful place, where you are 'Alive' and free, spread the word!

No, I do not mean preach it until nobody wants to speak to you ever again. I mean, shine like the star you are, and people will wonder what you are doing differently. And if you want to help and inspire others, maybe start your own Instagram channel and join the Sober Movement! We are a friendly, collaborative bunch of people. And our numbers are ever growing. Your message might be the one that helps a struggling person get through their day.

And if that is not enough for you, then why not train to be an Alcohol Freedom Coach with *This Naked Mind*? There are course placements awarded annually at the time of writing. Reach out to me by email to find out more.

Let me know your thoughts on this book

I am not finished yet, and I won't be until our kids and our grandkids can walk into an event and not be questioned if they do not want to drink, or feel pressurised to do so. Until alcohol is treated much like smoking is now. Did you know that when I started my first job in a corporate setting, people were allowed to smoke in the office right next to us? Unbelievable now, of course. I hope alcohol will be a lot like this soon. The number one thing I would love to see is for alcohol advertising to be completely banned.

Drop me an email and let me know what you think of this book, whether it helped you, and suggestions for the next book, if you like.

And if this book has helped, even a little bit, then please leave a review? If it's a good one it will make my day, and I will know I helped another soul. It keeps me going on my path to undo all the damage alcohol does to us when we are most in need. ♥

Love and hugs,

Amanda x

Aka Zerofierce

TNMI Certified Alcohol Freedom Coach & ALP Practitioner

www.zerofierce.com

END CREDITS

A big thank you to my wonderful family, Steve, Levi, and Charlie. I love you all so much. I am so lucky to have you guys in my world.

Thank you for your patience when all I did was work, and thank you for allowing me the space to write freely, and get the book written. Now you can have the living room back, on occasion. Maybe. Unless of course I start another book... Actually - let me think about it, yeh?

To Tracey and Neil, my besties, for putting up with all my drivel as I set up my business and started telling the world how wonderful it was to live alcohol free. You both absolutely rock. And you never once accused me of preaching. Even though you live miles away, I will see you soon! I will never forget when you showed me all your AF drinks with pride when I popped round to see you both. Your support is so appreciated. I love you! Mwah!

To Charlie & Kate, for updating me about Insta reels, and TikTok, and for believing in me the minute I told you my plans. And for being my practice stooges during my exams. Especially you, Kate, for being so bloody brave. You are both awesome, and you, and your brother Levi, have been through a lot.

To Neil, my littlest baby brother, for being there when I most needed someone to come to the scary hospital visits with me to see

Alex. Thank you for putting up with my music in the car, without moaning about it even once. Not even when I played trance all week. And for listening to me drone on about my ZeroFierce dreams. And for not moaning at me for trying to find all the alcohol free options in Brighton bars. Love you!

A massive thank you also to team Digital UK at my workplace as I was writing this - Chris, for being an ever-patient and quite lovely boss, and for not firing me even when I probably deserved it. Mike, just for being supportive, incredible, wonderful you. Marwan for not rolling your eyes at me *too* much, and for all the hugs, and for the times we dressed in a complimentary fashion. And Gavin, for reading the book. I thought you might just throw it away, so thank you. To all four of you for taking part in my surveys for the book. You are all awesome. I told you I would mention you all. And now I have. Fame!

To Darren, Michelle, Tululah, Terry, Mel & Mel, Alberto, Max, Steven, Lara, Toni, and Chrissy. For putting up with me being a weirdo at work, and still being my very good friends. To Isabelle for accepting me as a Social Media Manager at Loaves of Love when I needed to discover myself a little more. And for letting me choose my job title. It meant a lot back then :)

To everyone in *World of Warcraft* Guilds *As Good As It Gets* and *Mystic Daggers* in *Azjol-Nerub* EU for being totally effing awesome human beings. And for all the other guilds for allowing me to play Holy Priest, even though Discipline was the preferred way to heal at the time. The best years of my life were never lost because I got to spend them with you. "B Team FTW!"

A huge thank you also to my fellow students and coaches at the *This Naked Mind* Institute. To my classmates who reviewed my book cover and topic study - Martha, Stacey, Paul the DJ, Doctor Jenie, Laura, Nikki, Marcin, Jeanette & Michelle. To my perfect housemates in Tampa, Judi, Shay, and Sue - thank you for reading the draft copies. To Jess for being my apostrophe Queen, and for removing as many of the Oxford commas as I would allow. To fellow students Maria, Courtney, Cari, Kelly, Milagros, Justine, Barry, Nicole, Adam, Jen, Laura, Joan, Sammie, Angela, Vanessa, and Paul the artist. To Mike, Onowa, Pam, Hillary, Hayley, Zoe, and Cole for all the fantastic coaching and your brilliant training. To Eryn and Dorothy for having me in their ALP group. To all my fellow coaches for supporting ZeroFierce, for believing in me, and for being so damn huggable in Tampa. You are all remarkable. I am honoured and privileged to walk with you on this journey to change the world.

To Sally, from Rebalance by Sally, my menopause coach, who I hired after I had given up drinking. You told me I could do it all. Turns out you were right! My gratitude to you, lovely human. Thank you for helping me to believe in me again. And for telling me I had not gone mad.

To Annie Grace, who is probably the smartest person I have *ever* met, for creating *This Naked Mind*, and for your tireless study for us all. And thank you to Annie's whole team of awesome people at *This Naked Mind*, especially Pam, for being our rock and our champion throughout. We all love you so much, Pam.

Thank you to every single one of you for your follows on social media, email subscribes, blog reads, thank you emails, and support, and for all your words of encouragement. Thank you to all my clients for reaching out and saying thank you when I got it right. It spurred me on! Thank you for reading this book. I appreciate you *all* so much.

And to all of you who have so far reached out to me for help with alcohol, **YOU are the warriors, the bravest of the brave.** You are my favourite people on this planet. **Together, we *will* change the world.**

And most of all, heavenly hugs to my perfect son, Daniel, George (my Dad), Maureen (my Mum), our bestie Terry, more of Steve's childhood friends Craig and James, my work friends Carole and Jayne, and to my brother, Alex. All of you were taken too soon. I love you all to the moon and back, and I did all of this for you. ♥

About The Author

Amanda Foster is an Alcohol & Addiction Freedom Coach and Digital Marketer based in a sleepy island on the South Coast of England called Hayling Island. She is the Founder of ZeroFierce which has helped countless people break free from the chains of alcohol addiction and find lasting peace. She also helps other freedom coaches with their website, digital marketing, and social media fears.

Often asked why ZeroFierce, she explains:

Zero, because zero alcohol.

"Fierce, because I like to throw rocks at our enemies, those being largely Big Alcohol. Unless they make alcohol free drinks, in which case I throw a little sand instead."

When asked if she hates alcohol, she says:

"No, I do not hate alcohol. It drives my hybrid car beautifully, and makes for a great hand sanitiser."

When out and about at parties, she is often asked if she minds people drinking near her. To which she will reply:

"Not at all. See you in ten years."

You can get in touch with Amanda via her website at:

www.zerofierce.com

Email her: Amanda@zerofierce.com

Follow her on Instagram:

https://www.instagram.com/zerofierce/

Or Facebook: https://www.facebook.com/zerofierce

For lots of alcohol-free resources, sign up for emails here:

https://www.zerofierce.com/free-ebook

New book coming soon - ETA November 2024!

Printed in Dunstable, United Kingdom